Young Peacemakers
Project Book

Young Peacemakers
Project Book

Kathleen M. Fry-Miller
Judith A. Myers-Walls

Illustrations by
Janet R. Domer-Shank

Foreword by
Kathleen and James McGinnis

BRETHREN PRESS
Elgin, Illinois

Young Peacemakers Project Book

BRETHREN PRESS, 1451 Dundee Avenue,
Elgin, Illinois 60120

Illustrations by Janet R. Domer-Shank
Cover art by Vista III

Library of Congress Cataloging in Publication Data

Fry-Miller, Kathleen.
     Young peacemakers project book.

     Includes bibliographies and index.
     Summary: Includes instructions for a variety of projects that promote peace and concern for the environment.
        1. Peace—Juvenile literature.   2. Environmental protection—Juvenile literature.   [1. Peace.
2. Environmental protection]   I. Myers-Walls, Judith.
II. Title.
JX1963.F87   1988   327.1'72   88-7328
ISBN 0-87178-976-0

Manufactured in the United States of America

Everybody can be great. Because anybody can serve. You don't have to have a college degree to serve. You don't have to make your subject and your verb agree to serve . . . You only need a heart full of grace. A soul generated by love.

Martin Luther King, Jr.

We dedicate this book to our children,

Eric, Amy, and Carrie Fry-Miller,

Amanda and Aaron Myers-Walls,

Neil, Drew, and Reed Domer-Shank,

and all children.

You are our inspiration, our purpose,

and our future.

Many thanks to Paul, Dick, and Kenton

for your patience and loving support.

Contents

Foreword

"Peace must be built; it must be
built up every day by works of peace."

Those words by Pope Paul VI have always lifted up for us two crucial ingredients in peacemaking—perseverance and possibility. Perseverance implies that the task is a long-term one, that the fruits are not always immediately discernible, but that we will indeed be given the strength to sustain us. Possibility means that there is hope; hope that lies not only in an overview of the potential for peace in the world but also in the fact that there are specific concrete actions we can take in our own everyday lives to make peace more of a daily reality. This book by Fry-Miller and Myers-Walls is an exciting example of the perseverance and the possibility that should inform all peacemaking efforts, especially those efforts undertaken in the company of children.

We would wager that anyone reading this book does not need to be convinced of the importance as well as the urgency of peacemaking efforts in today's world. The question is not usually "why?" but "how?"

Several crucial strategies in educating for peacemaking are exemplified in innovative ways in this book.

First, *peacemaking needs to be the art of the possible. People must be affirmed in what they are already doing before they can conceive of moving on to anything else.*

Fry-Miller and Myers-Walls have compiled a wealth of activities that are not only doable for children but also for the adults who are working with the children, either as parents or as teachers. Adults will very quickly be able to see that many of the activities they are already doing with children are indeed "peacemaking" activities. They will also see that slight variations or new questions posed to children can enhance the peacemaking quality of a more standard activity. For example, a bread-baking activity can be followed by a discussion question for the children about what it would be like to live on a very simple diet of rice, beans, and bread, as do many people of the world.

The authors also have a clear understanding of developmental concerns; therefore, they are careful to differentiate between suggestions for very young children and for children at the top of their age range (10 years). This kind of specification is yet another way of making the activity itself more possible.

Secondly, *peace educators must model the world they are seeking to create both in the content and in the methodology of their educational activities.* This kind of modeling jumps out of the pages of this book. Every suggested activity is inherently respectful of the resources of the earth and of the fact that expensive materials are not available to all educators or all families. Therefore these suggestions are not ones that offer opportunities only to those with economic resources. Cooperation is stressed, both in the content of the activities them-selves and in the process. The children are encouraged to think of others and to work together on many different levels. The whole idea of the importance of friendship and building relations with others is also integral to the activities. This relationship-building includes suggestions for activities with older people, grandparents or other older adults in the community, as well as with the children's peers.

One last consideration with regard to being a model relates to the question of the "examined life." It seems to us that it's essential to lay the basis in early years for children's development of their critical thinking skills. They also need to be encouraged to look at what they are thinking and doing with an analytical eye. Many of the activities in this book help children do just that. Questions like "What happens to things if they are not recycled?", "Can you think of any ways to use paper bags to save energy?", "How does it feel to be able to tell someone about your feelings?", "What's not fun about playing war?", help children think about actions that they may otherwise take for granted.

A third important strategy for peacemaking is *nurturing of compassion in different areas of the children's lives.* The authors of this book have offered a wide range of possibilities for encouraging the growth of a caring spirit in a child—from appreciating a "backyard zoo" to fixing special treats for bird friends, to "adopting a grandparent," to collecting food for a local food bank. A compassionate heart is nurtured in many ways and at many levels with young children. They need to be constantly called to go beyond themselves and their immediate concerns. The more their lives are touched by people who are hurting—whether through stories or personal contact—as well as by people and animals who need their care, the greater their capacity for compassion will be.

A fourth strategy is based on the reality that *all of us are moved by the lives and stories of people who are working for change.* Fry-Miller and Myers-Walls talk about peace heroes and about celebrating their birthdays or the special days of some of these heroes. Whether they are called "new-day" or "new age" heroes or "peace heroes," the message is the same. These are people who have worked and continue to work for a world where people live together in a just and violence-free society. Our children desperately need to know the stories of people who live for others and who often do so at great risk. Unfortunately, today a child's concept of hero is influen-ced dramatically by the kinds of heroes that fill the T.V. screens—generally people of power who do not hesitate to use violence. This kind of constant exposure makes it even more important to introduce children to a different kind of hero.

Lastly, *peacemaking must be a joy-filled endeavor.* Much of the work of peace seems to be ominous, oppressive, and so serious. It is critical for those of us who work with children to show them by our actions, by our smiles, and by the activities we encourage them to do that peacemak-ing is *fun.* It is a life-style filled with joy, hope, and humor, As the old saying goes, "If the love of God is in your heart, there is a smile on your face." If children do not see joy mirrored in our peace actions, they will certainly not be attracted to being peacemakers, especially for the long haul.

The authors of this book excel in their ability to encourage a sense of wonder in children and to develop in myriad ways the imagination and creativity that are innate in children but need to be called forth. The readers of this book will be struck by a wonderful sense of hope, of life, of fun, of an imaginative faithfulness. They will indeed be able to say with conviction,

"Peace is possible."

Kathleen and James McGinnis
Parenting for Peace and Justice Network
St. Louis, Missouri

Introduction

Building Bridges of Understanding and Hope

These are challenging times. People across the United States joined forces to create a peace ribbon to wrap around the Pentagon. Panels of the ribbon are displayed in the Smithsonian and other sections of the ribbon have been shared in many countries. At the same time the all-volunteer U.S. Armed Forces advertise military service as an educational world tour, and the production and sales of war toys have skyrocketed. The song "We Are the World" has brought millions of people of all ages in many countries together to raise resources and awareness about hunger and spawned numerous similar projects, while G. I. Joe has regained popularity as a children's toy and has been made into a nationally broadcast cartoon. It appears that the forces of peace are gaining new strength and momentum at the same time that war is being revived as a glorious and patriotic event. For children this revival of war means that a seemingly endless variety of war play equipment and related characters have bombarded them in the toy store, on television, in comic books, and in many other aspects of their lives.

Other complexities of today's world face children and families as well: some children—and some adults—find that computer technology makes establishing relationships with machines easier than with people; natural wilderness and even the safety of city drinking water are in jeopardy as technologically advanced nations search for the energy to maintain their industries and individual life styles and for ways to dispose of the wastes produced by their wealth; major powers attempt to find ways to reduce worldwide stores of nuclear arms at the same time as they increase their own current number of warheads. Some Christians believe the teachings of Jesus about nonviolence are central to the faith and try to live by them, while others, including a number of ministers-turned-politicians, advocate a strong military build-up and present a God-is-on-our-side philosophy.

Even the world immediately surrounding the children is complex and changing. Many more children than ever before are being cared for by adults who are not their parents for at least a portion of the day. Many live in single-parent homes. At an early age many begin to care for themselves at the same time that the safety of children has become a major concern. The media explosions of the "information age" provide children with visions of current events and access to facts and figures that are overwhelming to adults, let alone to children. In the face of all of these situations, child development experts have stated that the development of pro-social behavior—the ability to deal effectively with others— may be the most important task of parents, caregivers, and teachers responsible for helping children become competent adults.

Parents and teachers are faced with a number of challenges during these times: How can they help children learn sensitivity and concern for others in this age of computer technology?

How can they encourage them to cherish and protect the earth's natural resources in a way that enhances the quality of life for all people? How can they teach the application of religious principles to everyday life when public figures present so many conflicting interpretations of how that is done? How can they help children develop values of peace and justice as they cope with the flood of information facing them? How can they provide children with the sense of belonging and acceptance usually accompanying family life when broken relationships are a part of their family tree? How can they help to lay the groundwork for children to lead constructive lives in a world they will come to know is besieged with war and threatened with nuclear extinction?

Peace Education Provides an Answer

Peacemaking projects, like those presented here, can provide important tools to parents and teachers as they try to help children grow up in a very complex world. This book presents fun, creative activities for children and parents or teachers to do together. They are not simply fun activities, however. They were chosen and designed to provide children with education about peace. The peace focus is important for several reasons. First, children are concerned about war. Researchers have shown that children as young as six and possibly younger know enough about nuclear war to associate the word "nuclear" with death and suffering. A second reason to focus on peace was mentioned briefly earlier; peacemaking skills have been related to overall child competence. These skills include understanding and caring about another person's point of view, dealing creatively with conflict, making and keeping friends, and working cooperatively with others. A third reason to teach peace to children is to balance out the forces in our world (including media) which are actively teaching the principles of war and destruction. Even parents and teachers who do not consider themselves pacifists or peace educators are concerned about passing on values of helpfulness and cooperation to their children. A fourth reason to help children to become peacemakers is because the threats to peace and justice are real. The possibility of nuclear extinction of all life on this planet in a moment hangs over us at all times. For millions of children life is a daily struggle against poverty and war. By educating children in the ways of peace, parents and teachers become peace advocates themselves, as well as laying the groundwork for tomorrow's decision-makers to work toward a more peaceful and socially just world.

There are four guiding principles for these projects that should make them useful tools. First, each activity is designed to build the child's understanding of an issue related to peace. Second, the activities introduce the language, concepts, and characters of peace. Third, the projects aim at building self-esteem and providing a means for children to have an impact on their world. Fourth, the activities attempt to demonstrate that creation and cooperation can be fun.

About the Structure of this Book

The *Young Peacemakers Project Book* is structured to make it easy for children to take a lead in choosing the activity they would like to complete. The illustrated "recipes" provide the child with an idea of what each activity involves. For the parent or teacher working with one or more children there is a background section at the beginning of each chapter that describes the importance of the activities in that chapter and their relationship to peace issues. The chapter introduction also includes the objectives which are addressed by the activities in that chapter. The text describing each activity has been written at a level that should be understandable to children aged 3 to 10 when it is read to them. Older children in that age group will be able to read the words themselves. Although children will be able to complete many of the tasks with a certain amount of independence, it is hoped that parents or teachers will join with the children to complete the activities cooperatively. Such involvement will both increase the effectiveness of the teaching and provide an opportunity for strengthening the adult-child relationships. We also believe that adults will enjoy the projects almost as much as the children! Those activities or steps of activities that require adult guidance for safety reasons or because the task is too difficult for children to accomplish on their own is marked with this symbol: *A* (for Adult).

Appropriate Age Levels

These activities were designed for children aged three to ten years. We hope that most children of those ages will find the activities enjoyable and will be able to understand, or at least begin to understand, many of the ideas being presented. Activities which are definitely too difficult for most younger children are marked with this symbol: *O* (for Older child). Because the 3 to 10 age range is a broad one, it is important to understand the differences among children of those ages and present the activities appropriately. For our purposes here, the children can be grouped roughly into three categories: preschool (approximately 3–5 years); early elementary (approximately 5–8 years); and late elementary (approximately 8–10 years).

Preschool children can do simple activities that do not take long periods of concentration. They should be able to see immediate results and should not be required to do anything that involves complex skills. The children should be challenged, but can become frustrated easily. They will need close, step-by-step guidance and hands-on experiences that allow them to see, hear, touch, taste, and smell. Adults should be ready to help with the more complex aspects of the activity, but should not take over in the areas in which the child is competent. For example, a number of the activities involve working with pictures from magazines. Adults may need to cut the pictures out, but the preschooler can choose which pictures to use and can glue them on a page. Where written stories, poems, lists, and messages are a part of the activity, adults will need to write the words that the child dictates. A simple statement of the values and ideas behind the projects can be introduced, but adults should hold realistic expectations for how much preschoolers will understand. Listen carefully to their comments as they try to put these complex ideas into words that they can comprehend.

Early elementary children, on the other hand, will be able to be more independent with the projects. They will begin to be able to read some of the descriptions themselves and, perhaps, do some of their own writing. They will be able to plan for the projects by gathering materials, helping to prepare the work area, and working around the schedules of friends, classmates, and family. They are developing more skills and will be able to do more complicated tasks, but they still will need much guidance, especially when the task is new. Progress with projects should be noticeable to these children in one or two sessions. At this age the "Let's Talk About It" questions can be especially helpful in leading the child toward an understanding of concepts behind the activities. Children may bring a real creativity to the projects at this age and may suggest some exciting alternatives to the written descriptions.

Late elementary children will be able to read the project descriptions and will be able to complete many of the tasks with little or no adult instruction. They may want to do the activities entirely on their own, but we encourage parents and teachers to discover ways that the children can work beside the adults rather than under their supervision. Adults may need to help the children interpret what they are reading and help to make decisions about the appropriateness of the chosen activity considering available time and resources. Late elementary children will be able to grasp most of the concepts and values behind the activity, and adults can help them explore those thoughts further and apply them to related situations. Children of this age also will be able to go beyond the activity to other projects of their own creation, will be able to think of alternative ways of completing the tasks, and will be able to think of implications beyond those represented in the "Let's Talk About It" sections. This can be an exciting time for the adults as well as for the young people!

Another important point related to age is that these activities provide a rich opportunity for working with multiple age groups. Older children can help the younger ones with the tasks. Younger children can share their excitement and sense of wonder with the older ones. Older children can increase their understanding of the concepts by explaining them to the younger ones, which helps the younger ones, too. Young people who may feel they are "too old" to participate in the activities may benefit from helping to direct a younger group in their completion. Flexibility is the key; use your imagination and consult your own expertise in working with children.

About the Targeted Audience

Beyond being useful to different ages, this book should be useful to a variety of types of audiences. Families can use it for family activity times, for rainy days, and for times when little ones say, "I don't have anything to do." Or they may want to work through the book systematically on a regular basis. In these ways, parents may make it a part of their own peace education efforts.

Teachers, leaders, and other adults in nursery schools, child care homes and centers, after-school activity programs (including youth programs such as Scouts, Camp Fire, and 4-H), parochial and public schools may find it provides just the thing for new approaches to art and nature projects and to the teaching of basic human interaction skills. Preschool teachers may find that the chapter structure will work well in providing weekly or monthly themes. Some activities can be used for interest areas, and others can be whole group activities.

Youth group leaders working with young people on a once-a-week basis may want to choose one chapter at a time to work on, or may want to choose just one activity out of each chapter. As was mentioned above, the activities are appropriate for both single-age and multi-age groupings of children.

This may be just the book for the Sunday school teacher looking for action-oriented projects for Sunday morning. Many of the projects or the tasks which are part of them can be done in one or more short time periods (15 minutes to a half an hour), and can be completed with different types of groupings of children. Sunday school teachers and other religious trainers may want to use Bible verses as the basis for each activity. (Some suggested verses for each section appear at the end of the book.)

About the Authors and Illustrator

The authors and illustrator have roots in the Church of the Brethren, a denomination known as one of the historic peace churches. Our commitment to peace, our first instruction in peace, and our fellowship with other peacemakers all originated in that upbringing. Christianity provided the basis for us in this endeavor, but there are other bases as well. All three of us have an educational and employment background related to child development. We all have extensive experience in the out-of-doors. All three of us are parents. We assume that, in a similar way, the readers of this book will bring a variety of philosophical, religious, and experiential backgrounds to their use of the projects. This assumption has led us to design activities so that they may be used in both religious settings—Protestant, Catholic, Jewish, or other faiths—and in secular settings as well.

We have provided a structure and the beginning. You can take it from there. Use the *Project Book* to become part of a global climate where adults and children can work actively together with great hope and deep commitment toward building a world in which "swords are turned into plowshares and spears into pruning hooks." Have fun, and may peace be with you!

Kathleen Fry-Miller
Fort Wayne, Indiana

Judith Myers-Walls
West Lafayette, Indiana

Section I
Caring for the Environment

1

Nature Wonders

Background information:

The world is a complex, interdependent system. People and other animals depend on the earth for food, for an atmosphere that provides air and a comfortable temperature range, for materials for shelter, for many sources of energy, and for an environment that provides opportunities for learning, having fun, and dealing with other living beings. Plants and other life forms require many of the same kinds of resources from earth. The earth depends on the ability of humans to care for its delicate balance with concern and respect. People now possess the ability to destroy the earth and its resources if they do not show that concern and respect.

An important part of becoming a peacemaker is learning to understand and live in harmony with nature. A tendency of people to assume an attitude of superiority and greater importance than other aspects of the earth leads to a misuse and squandering of its resources. The same results can occur as a result of taking the natural environment for granted. Plants and animals along with nonliving aspects of the environment experience continual violence and intervention from humans. Children should learn to protect and care for nature in the process of learning to value life and creation. Such learning will nurture them in their growth as effective peacemakers. In addition, because young children spend much of their lives being cared for, they need opportunities to learn to care for others. Caring for animals or even plants that need help can begin to make children feel nurturant and important. And living in harmony with the environment is an essential part of living in harmony with other people.

As an attempt to help children develop a sense of wonder and an appreciation of their role as caregiver for the environment, the activities in this chapter give children an opportunity to experience nature firsthand. In all cases the activities are structured to emphasize the interdependence of humans and nature.

Objectives

For Young Children:

- To use their senses to experience nature and the environment around them.
- To begin to explore the difference between items which are manufactured or produced by people and those which are natural.
- To build on their learning of colors, shapes, and sizes.
- To begin to define the concepts of living and nonliving.
- To begin to take a role in caring for animals.

For Early Elementary Children:

- To use their knowledge of nature to interpret what they see and hear in the environment around them.
- To begin to learn the concepts of "conservation" and "endangered wildlife."
- To refine their understanding of the concepts of living, no longer living, and nonliving.
- To explore the differences among life forms in the ground, in water, and in the air and how they differ between seasons and times of day.
- To make some progress toward taking responsibility for the care of another being and learn to become reliable at the task.

For Later Elementary Children

- To slow down enough to use their senses to experience a quiet environment.
- To explore some of the implications of not using conservation techniques in dealing with the environment.
- To begin to identify several types of plants and animals in several settings.
- To explore the interrelationship of water, forest, and other ecological systems.

For All Children:

- To sharpen observation skills.
- To cultivate their sense of wonder about the environment.
- To feel at home with nature.
- To use their creativity to express their understanding and appreciation of nature to other people.
- To learn to care for the environment.

Outdoor Adventure

Nature Walk

What To Do:

Take a walk. Go someplace without many people or buildings. Try a park, a woods, or an open field. Walk for a while. Then stop. Relax and breathe slowly. Look for things from nature. Look, listen, touch, and smell. Watch quietly for hidden wildlife. Listen to the sounds. Close your eyes and be very still.

Backyard Zoo

What To Do:

In your own backyard or a nearby park, take a slow walk. Look for places where you might find creatures (little animals or bugs) hiding. Look in sidewalk cracks, under rocks or logs, in the air, under plants, or behind bushes. Watch quietly and be careful not to bother the creatures that you find.

Puddles, Streams, and Water Holes

You Will Need:

- Plastic wrap
- Can opener or scissors
- tin can or milk carton
- water—a puddle, stream, lake, or ocean
- rubber band

What To Do:

1. Make an underwater viewer. Open both ends of the tin can or milk carton. Put the plastic wrap over one end of the container. Hold it in place with a rubber band.

2. Take your viewer to the nearest puddle, stream, lake, or ocean. Put the plastic-covered end into the water and look. You may want to put on old boots or tennis shoes for a creek walk. Remember to be very still to see the animals in the water.

Let's Talk About It:

What did you see? What things were moving? What things were still? What creatures did you see?

What did you smell and feel? What sounds did you hear?

Could you tell which things that you saw and heard were from nature and which were made by people? What are the differences? How can you tell?

Other Things To Do:

Pick up nature items that are on the ground while you walk. Put them in a paper bag. Do not hurt living trees, flowers, and plants. Look closely at the objects. Sort them by color, texture, or type of object. Save them for art projects.

A Take a walk after dark, in different kinds of weather, or in different seasons. How are the sounds, smells, and colors different?

Paint or draw a picture of your outdoor adventures. Tell a story or make up a poem about nature.

Use guidebooks to learn the names of trees, wildflowers, bugs, or animals.

O Find out about plants or animals that are endangered. Learn what endangered means and why it happens.

Nature Art

Collage

You Will Need:
- nature items
- cardboard or paper
- glue or wire

What To Do:
1. Collect nature items to use for your collage. You can always add as you work on the collage.

2. Glue the items onto your paper or cardboard.

3. For heavier objects, twist wire around the object. Then stick the ends of the wire through the cardboard or paper.

Sculpture

You Will Need:
- nature items
- salt
- flour
- water
- small bowl
- measuring cups and spoons
- a small piece of cardboard OR a plastic lid

What To Do:

1. Make salt dough. Put 2 cups of flour, 1 cup of salt, and 1 cup of water in the small bowl. Mix it. Then knead it (push on it with both hands) for 10 minutes.

2. Put a handful of salt dough onto the lid or cardboard.

3. Stick and poke and arrange nature objects in the dough. Then set your sculpture aside to get hard.

Mobile

You Will Need:
- nature items   • a branch   • string

What To Do:
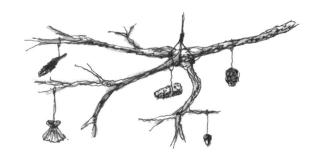
1. *A* Tie one end of a string to each nature item you choose.
3. Tie the other end of the string to the branch.
4. Hang the branch and watch the mobile turn and move.

Pictures and Books

You Will Need:
- nature items   • paper   • glue   • wax paper   • an iron
- crayons or markers   • a stapler or string

What To Do:
1. Make pictures from nature items. You could:

Find some flat objects, like leaves or grass. Glue them onto paper.

Pull off two pieces of wax paper. Find leaves, flowers, grass, or other flat things from nature. Arrange the items in between the pieces of wax paper. *A* Turn the iron on low. Iron the paper gently so that the sides stick together.

Put pieces of paper on top of items from nature. Rub the paper with a crayon to see the pattern of the nature item.

2. You could collect the pages you have made. You may want to write the names of the nature items on the pictures. Maybe you could tell a story with the pages.
3. Staple your book together, or punch holes in the pages and tie it together.

Nature Moves and So Can You

You Will Need:
- • yourself
- • your imagination

What To Do:

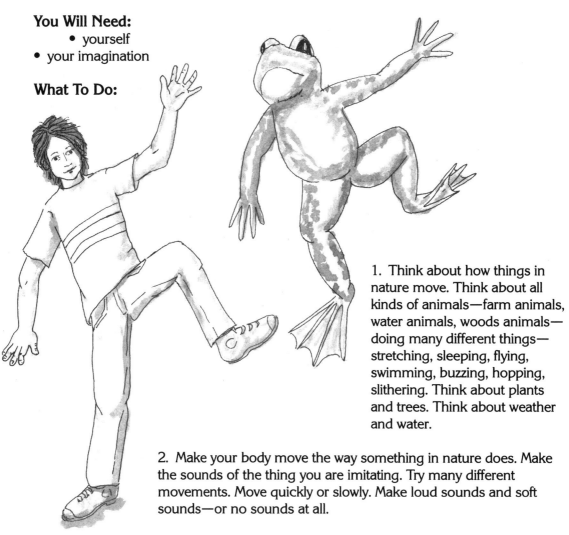

1. Think about how things in nature move. Think about all kinds of animals—farm animals, water animals, woods animals— doing many different things— stretching, sleeping, flying, swimming, buzzing, hopping, slithering. Think about plants and trees. Think about weather and water.

2. Make your body move the way something in nature does. Make the sounds of the thing you are imitating. Try many different movements. Move quickly or slowly. Make loud sounds and soft sounds—or no sounds at all.

Let's Talk About It:

Which ideas were easy to make? Which were hard? Are they easy or hard for the thing you were imitating? How many different ways can you move your body?

Other Things To Do:

Take turns imitating something. Have your friends or family guess what you are imitating.

Play Follow-the-Leader with one person choosing and leading a motion and others following.

Create a story and act it out using the many nature movements and sounds that you have been learning about.

O Learn bird calls. See if you can get birds to answer your calls.

Bird Friends

Pine Cone Treats

You Will Need:
- pine cones with a string tied to each
- vegetable shortening
- newspapers
- two flat pans
- bird seed or dried bread crumbs

What To Do:
1. Cover a table with newspaper. Spread the shortening in one flat pan. Put the bird seed or bread crumbs in the other pan.

2. Roll a pine cone in the shortening, and then in the bird seed.

3. Hang the bird feeder on a tree, bush, or fence. Watch the birds from a window.

Let's Talk About It:
Why do you think it is hard for the birds to find food in the winter? What do birds eat if we do not feed them?

Why do we hang the food up high? How do the birds reach it? What happens when we get too noisy while we are watching the birds?

What other animals do people help to feed?

Other Things To Do:
Use round cereal with a hole in the middle and stiff string to "string O's." Tie one piece on the end of the string so the other pieces do not slip off. Hang the string outside.

Make a "Happy Holidays" dinner for the birds. Use a needle and thread to string cranberries and popcorn.

Watch the birds while they eat. Watch them fly away and come back for more. Where do you think they go?

Learn the names of different kinds of birds. You might want to make your own bird or winter animals book by making drawings of those different kinds that you see in your own yard.

Feed the birds often in winter. It is especially important after a snow. Your bird friends will start to count on you.

2
Litterbugs Beware

Background information:

This chapter continues the theme of caring for the environment. Litter is something even young children can see and understand. Just as they learn that cleaning up the environment inside a home is important, they can begin to learn to clean up the world around them by putting trash in its proper place. Air and water pollution are much less concrete, but the activities here attempt to make the concepts less abstract.

Keeping the environment clean requires two primary elements from an individual. First is an awareness of one's own behavior and how it impacts the environment. Absent-minded discarding of trash can become a difficult habit to break. The second is an ownership and caring about the world and its air, water, open places and hidden spaces. Children often feel that what they do has little or no impact on others, so these activities both emphasize the negative effect of littering and pollution and provide some opportunities to have a positive influence on their surroundings by reducing the amount of pollution or litter.

Objectives

For Young Children:
- To define litter and begin to notice it.
- To begin to categorize types of discarded material.
- To consider the concepts of air and water pollution.

For Early Elementary Children:
- To plan and carry out a project related to litter control.
- To understand the concept of decomposition and how various materials are effected by it.
- To explore the concepts of air and water pollution and how they are related to the observable surroundings.

For Later Elementary Children:

- To understand the impact of decomposition of litter on the environment.
- To plan and carry out an environmental experiment.
- To explore public policy policy issues related to litter and pollution.

For All Children:

- To build an awareness of the presence of litter and pollution.
- To develop a sense of ownership of and responsibility for the environment.

No More Litterbugs

You Will Need:
- a paper bag or trash bag
- some friends
- a wagon (if you want it)
- old gloves (if you want them)

What To Do:

1. Find an area outside that you want to clean up. It could be your yard, the schoolyard, or an area of a park. The more people you have, the bigger the area you can clean up.

2. Carefully put any pieces of litter that you find into your bags or wagon. You might find papers, cans, bottles, and other things. Do not pick up broken glass without gloves on.

3. Put your trash in a trash can. Recycle cans and bottles if you can. Ask your friends and family to always use trash containers to keep the earth beautiful. No more litterbugs!

Let's Talk About It:

Where does litter come from?

Why is it important to keep our earth looking clean?

What things can you do each day to help out?

Do some places have more litter than others? Do different places have different kinds of litter? Talk about some of the reasons for more litter some places, such as being close to a fast food restaurant, crowded living conditions, or out-of-the-way places like roadside ditches or alleys.

Do some kind of litter (like glass and styrofoam) seem to last forever on the ground? Do other kinds of litter (like paper and garbage) fall apart after a few weeks?

Other Things To Do:

Pick other areas that you would like to see cleaned up. You might want to do litter collecting on a regular basis.

A Find out which areas of your city or county have workers that keep them cleaned. Find out where help is needed.

A Think of a place with lots of litter. What could be done to help? Do people need signs to help them remember? Does the area need another trash can? Can you help to solve the problem?

A Make trash containers for people to carry in cars. Give them to friends and family. Maybe you could sell them as a group project.

A Make a poster about litter. The poster should show how you feel about litter or what people should do to stop the litter problem. Put the poster up in your school, church, or in a store.

O Help your family take out the trash. You could try weighing your trash to see how much your family throws out each week. How many pounds of trash would your town have each week if every family had as much trash as you?

Garbage Awareness Collage

You Will Need:
- your trash collection
- bags or boxes for sorting
- a large piece of corrugated cardboard
- glue and wire

What To Do:

1. Put your bags or boxes in a line. Put these words on the containers (or draw pictures on them):

Glass   Metal   Paper   Plastics and Styrofoam   Food Waste

Put each piece of trash in the right bag or box.

2. Draw lines on the cardboard to divide it into five sections. Write the same five words or draw the same five pictures on the cardboard, one in each section.

3. Glue pieces of trash onto the board. For heavier pieces, wrap wire around them. Then stick the wire through the cardboard.

4. *A* Take your collage to the people who make decisions in your neighborhood or town. Give them a letter saying where you found the litter and how you feel about it.

Let's Talk About It:

How did you decide which bag to put each piece of garbage in? Were there pieces that didn't fit? Did some pieces belong in more than one bag?

How can we help keep our earth clean? Who else needs to help?

Other Things To Do:

O You may want to sort the garbage into more categories. Maybe you could get it ready for recycling. For that you may need to separate colors of glass, types of metal or aluminum, or other groups.

A Put your collage up in different places to show more people how you feel about litter.

O Choose pieces of different kinds of garbage. Put some dirt in a large jar. Then put in some garbage, then stones. Make several layers and fill the jar with water. After a week empty the jar onto a garbage bag. What happened to the garbage? Look up the word "decomposition" in the dictionary. Talk about decomposition and litter.

Clean Air Test

You Will Need:

- wax paper
- scissors
- petroleum jelly

What To Do:

1. Cut the wax paper into four squares (or more). Rub a little petroleum jelly on each square.

2. Put the pieces of paper in different places. Try places inside your house, school, or church. Try the kitchen, near a heating vent or ducts, or near the door. Think of places outside, like close to a busy street, near a factory, or by a dusty road. Try to think of clean places, too. Check the pieces of paper after a day and after a week.

Let's Talk About It:

How did the papers look after a day? How did they look after a week? Why did they look that way? Where did the dirt come from?

Which place was the dirtiest? Which place was the cleanest? How were the kinds of dirt different?

How could the dirt in the air effect your body and your health?

Other Things To Do:

O Do this activity several days in a row. Put a new piece of paper in the same place each day. Watch the TV weather or look in the newspaper. See what they say about "air quality." Compare that rating with how your papers change from day to day.

O Talk with someone in charge of your city or county. Also talk to people, like members of environmental groups, who work to take care of our world. Ask them about pollution control and ways they are working to make our air cleaner. Ask what you can do to help.

Clean Water Test

You Will Need:

- coffee filters   • a strainer   • containers with lids

What To Do:

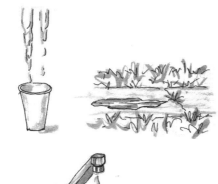

2. Put some of the water in a container. Put different kinds of water in different containers. Write on the containers where the water came from.

1. Find water in different places. You might find water in your sink, rain water, bath water, melted snow, creek or river water, or water from other places.

3. Put a coffee filter in the strainer. Put it over a bowl. Slowly pour each type of water into the coffee filter and strainer until it runs through. Pour out the water in the bowl.

4. Use a different filter for each type of water. Mark each filter with words or pictures. They should say where the water came from. Then when you are done, lay the coffee filters on a table. See how they look alike and different.

Let's Talk About It:

Which water seemed to be the cleanest? Which seemed to be the dirtiest? Why are they different?

Do some filters look dirty even though the water looked clean?

Is some dirt okay in drinking water?

Other Things To Do:

A Visit a water treatment plant to see how water is made clean for use in our homes, churches, and schools.

Invite someone that has a well to talk about how it works and what they do to keep their water clean.

Find out about some of the things that make water undrinkable that do not show up in a coffee filter. Find out how to test water for those things.

A Find out where your city or town gets its water. How clean is the water? Does your city or town need to be careful not to use too much water?

3

Use It Wisely, and Use It Again!

Background information:

Once children (and adults) have gained an awareness of the problems of litter and waste, what follows could be a sense of despair. Waste management is an overwhelming problem, as are many of the concerns related to peacemaking. But building hope and looking for solutions that are not easy or obvious are goals of peacemaking efforts. One step in this effort is exploring ways of saving energy. But there is hope even when dealing with waste. A promising management tool at this time in history is recycling.

The recycling of newspapers has been a traditional project for children. It is helpful if the project is seen as more than simply a way to make money, however. Children who understand the reasons for recycling and generally how the process is accomplished may be more committed to the effort. The "Making Paper" project is an example of an activity that makes an abstract process real.

All of these efforts can introduce the idea of management of limited resources (such as energy, aluminum, and wood), which leads to a better understanding of the dilemmas related to the just sharing of the resources among individuals, geographic areas, and countries. So this chapter deals not only with the child's caring for the environment, but also begins to build an early understanding of one of the issues which creates problems in international relations.

Objectives

For Young Children:
- To begin to understand the idea of using items over instead of discarding them.
- To learn the word "recycle."
- To learn to sort items into major categories.

For Middle Elementary Children:
- To learn what kinds of materials can be recycled.
- To plan and carry out a system for recycling at home.
- To begin to understand the process of recycling.

For Later Elementary Children:

- To investigate community resources related to recycling.
- To organize a group in order to improve a community's recycling efforts.
- To plan and carry out a system for recycling at home.

For All Children:

- To become aware of energy use in everyday activities.
- To experience the power of the concept of recycling to overcome the despair of facing the waste management issue.
- To learn the procedures for recycling all possible items in their community.
- To build a sensitivity to the need for recycling.
- To use their creativity to think of ways to use items which are usually discarded.

Save Energy

You Will Need:
- paper
- pencil or crayons
- someone to write down your ideas (if you can't write yet)

What To Do:
1. Make a list or draw pictures of all the things around you that use fuel like gasoline, kerosene, natural gas, or electricity.

2. Think about how you can use your body to save energy. Think about other ways you can save energy. Make a list of your ideas to save energy. Draw pictures of your ideas, too. Then try your ideas. Remind your friends and family to do the things on your list, too.

Let's Talk About It:
Were you surprised how many things use fuel or electricity? Why is it important to use less fuel and electricity?

What energy-saving ideas are easy to remember to do? What things are harder to remember?

Think about the last time the electricity went off. What was that like? How do you think families did things before there was electricity and other fuels?

Other Things To Do:
Talk with grandparents or other older people and maybe people from other countries about how they do or did things without using much fuel or electricity. What was (is) life like for them? You may want to look for books with that kind of information.

A Start a "Save Energy" Campaign with your family, church, or school. Ask a grownup to help you compare utility or fuel bills before and after the campaign to see if you were able to make a difference.

O Find out how your electricity is made (generated). It could be from coal, nuclear energy, hydroelectric generators, or solar cells. Find out what the good and bad things are about making electricity that way.

Recycling Project

You Will Need:

- bags or boxes
- a place to keep filled bags or boxes
- a grown-up with a car

What To Do:

1. Find out what you can recycle in your community. Ask about glass, aluminum, newspapers, other metals, or anything else. Find out how to get the things ready to be recycled. Also find out where to take the things.

2. Collect the items that you can recycle in bags or boxes. Sort them or wash them if you need to. Remove labels if you need to.

3. Take your bags or boxes to the recycling center(s).

4. *A* If you get money for the things, you could think of how you might use the money in a helpful way. Think about giving it to a community project, or making a donation to your church or school.

Let's Talk About It:

What does "recycling" mean? What happens to things if they are not recycled? Why is recycling important?

Other Things To Do:

A Start a church, school, or neighborhood recycling project. Invite friends and other families to bring goods to a central collection space.

A Find out what happens to things after they are taken to the recycling center.

O If there are some things you cannot recycle in your town, see if you can change that. Work with friends and grown-ups to find out if you can start a recycling program for that item.

Talk with your family about how to make recycling easy. Find a system that makes it almost as easy to recycle as to throw things away.

A Find a place, like a soft drink machine, with many cans. Put a box or a can near the machine. Put a sign on the box asking people to put empty cans in it. Pick up the cans and take them to the recycling center often.

Make Your Own Paper

You Will Need:
- used, rough paper (like newspapers, paper towels, or newsprint)
- a deep bowl
- an electric mixer
- towels
- two pieces of thin, cotton cloth
- water
- an old catalogue
- your feet

What To Do:

1. Tear up the paper for recycling into small pieces.

2. Stuff the pieces into the bowl. Cover the paper with water. Let the bowl sit for two days. (Add more water if it starts to dry out.)

3. *A* Make pulp out of the soaked paper pieces and water using the electric mixer. Mix it for five minutes. (This will be messy!)

4. Lay out four layers of towels on top of each other. Put a piece of the cotton cloth on top. It is good to do this on the floor.

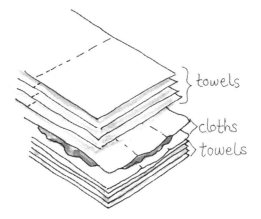

5. Spread some of the pulp onto the cloth. Use your fingers or a cup or strainer. Keep the pulp thin, but do not leave empty spaces.

6. Lay the other thin cloth on top, then add four more layers of towels. Pat the towels down, squeezing out some water.

7. Lay the catalogue on top. Stand on it for several minutes.

8. Lift up the towels and the cotton cloth. Carefully lift up your paper and lay it out to dry.

Other Things To Do:
   A Visit a plant that recycles paper to see what the process looks like on a large scale.
   Make different sizes of recycled paper.

Compost Jar

You Will Need:

- a large jar
- garden dirt
- houseplant fertilizer (with nitrogen)
- fruit and vegetable waste
- water

What To Do:

1. For several days save fruit and vegetable peelings and cores and what is left on plates at the end of a meal. (Do not save paper, bones, plastic, or meat scrapings.)

2. Put a layer of dirt in the bottom of the jar. Add a layer of food waste. Sprinkle some fertilizer on top. Repeat the layers until the jar is almost full. End with a layer of dirt. (Be sure to leave enough room to stir it.)

3. Keep the dirt damp, but not wet. Turn the contents of the jar over occasionally, about every week or two.

4. When you cannot see pieces of food in the mixture anymore, it is ready to put on your garden.

Let's Talk About It:

What do you think happened to the food?
Why do you think this will make good food for a garden?

Other Things To Do:

A Learn more about composting from books in the library or from the County Cooperative Extension Service. Learn which kinds of foods are good to add to a compost heap.

O Start a large compost heap in your back yard.

Recycling Brainstorm

You Will Need:

• paper bags   • your imagination

What To Do:

1. Think of all the different ways you can recycle paper bags instead of throwing them away. Think of ways to use them as bags, as paper, or as something else. Think of using them at your house, or giving them away to someone else. Think about useful things, pretty things, fun things, and silly things.

2. Try out at least three of your ideas.

Let's Talk About It:

Why do you think people usually just throw bags away?

Do any of your ideas save money for your family or someone else? Can you think of any ways to use bags to save energy?

Other Things To Do:

Think of ways to use other things you usually throw away.

Find out somewhere in your community where you can take broken appliances (like toasters and irons) instead of throwing them away. The next time something like that breaks at your house, help your parents remember to take it to be "recycled."

Find out places that will take used toys that children do not need any more. Help your parents go through your toy shelves to find things that you do not need or use anymore and that other children could use. Take the things to be "recycled."

Try the clothing recycling project in a later chapter.

Resource List

Caring For The Environment

Books:
Books for Young Children: The Natural Environment. Cooperative Extension publication NCR 123. (Available from Iowa and several midwest states.)

Cornell, Joseph Bharat. *Sharing Nature with Children: A Parents' and Teachers' Nature-Awareness Guidebook.* Nevada City, CA: Ananda Publications, 1979.

Diskin, Eve. *Yoga for Children.* New York: Warner Books, 1976.

Doan, Marlyn. *Starting Small in the Wilderness: The Sierra Club Outdoors Guide for Families.* San Francisco: Sierra Club Books, 1979.

Forte and Frank. *Puddles, Wings, and Grapevine Swings: Things to Make and Do with Nature's Treasures.* Nashville: Incentive Publications, 1982.

Golden Nature Guides: Birds, Flowers, Insects, Trees, Rocks and Minerals, Stars, Reptiles, Mammals, Fishes. New York: Western Publishing Co.

Graham, Bob. *The Junk Book: A Guide to Creative Uses of Recycled Materials for Children.* Distributed by Blanford Press, New York, 1986.

Katz, Adrienne. *Nature Watch: Exploring Nature With Your Children.* Redding, MA: Addison-Wesley, 1986.

Kelty, Jean McClure. *Adventures to Help Children Create a Humane World.* Youngstown, OH: George Whittell Memorial Press, 1982.

Rockwell, Robert, Elizabeth Sherwood, and Robert Williams. *Hug a Tree and Other Things to Do Outdoors With Young Children.* Mt. Rainier, MD: Gryphon House, 1983.

Wagner. *Solar Energy Education Packet for Elementary and Secondary Students.* Center for Renewable Resources (now Fund for Renewable Energy and the Environment), 1001 Connecticut Ave., N.W., Washington, D.C. 20036, 1979.

Children's Books:
Adams, Adrienne. *Poetry of Earth.*

Arnosky, Jim. *Deer at the Brook* and *O* *Secrets of a Wildlife Watcher.*

Bartlett, Margaret Farrington. *The Clean Brook.*

O Burleigh, Robert. *A Man Named Thoreau.*

Burton, Virginia Lee. *The Little House.*

Delton, Judy. *Walking With Dad on a Snowy Night.*

Dr. Suess. *The Lorax.*

Ets, Marie Hall. *Play with Me.*

Graham, Margaret Bloy. *Be Nice to Spiders.*

Hader, Berta and Elmer. *The Big Snow.*

Keats, Jack Ezra. *The Snowy Day.*

Krauss, Ruth. *The Carrot Seed.*

Schulevitz, Uri. *Dawn.*

Soya, Kiyoshi. *A House of Leaves.*

Children's Magazines:
Your Big Backyard and *Ranger Rick* from the Wildlife Federation, 8925 Leesburg Pike, Vienna, VA 22184-0001.

Organizations:
Concerned Educators Allied for a Safe Environment (CEASE)
c/o Peggy Schirmer
17 Gerry Street
Cambridge, MA 02138

Environmental T-Shirts
Jim Morris
P.O. Box 2308
Boulder, CO 80306

Fund for Renewable Energy and the Environment (FREE)
1001 Connecticut Ave. N.W.
Sixth Floor
Washington, D.C. 20036

National Geographic Society
17th and M Streets, N.W.
Washington, D.C. 20036

National Parks Association
Washington, D.C. 20005

National Wildlife Federation
1412 16th St. N.W.
Washington, D.C. 20036

Section II
Understanding People

4
No Two Are Alike

Background information:

The ability to care about others is based on the ability to care about oneself. Research has shown that positive self-concepts are related to many positive behaviors and accomplishments ranging from school achievement to the ability to make friends. In addition, support of others, tolerance, and the ability to identify positive aspects of people and situations have been found to be related to positive self-concepts.

The term "self-concept" is defined by different authors in different ways, but it is helpful to think of the trait as being made up of three components: self-image, self-esteem, and social identity. Self-image is the objective picture people have of themselves. It includes whether people consider themselves short or tall, chubby or thin, athletic or non-athletic, and red-headed or brunette. It is simply a description of oneself without evaluation. Self-esteem is the evaluation a person gives to the self-image. So it would include whether people think of themselves as *too* tall, *too* heavy, or as not athletic enough. Finally, social identity is the way people feel social groups to which they belong are perceived by society. Social identity could lead some red-heads to see themselves as being expected to be emotional and easily angered. Sex roles, racial biases, and age biases are also a part of this segment of self-concept.

Much of one's self-concept is based on the feeling of being unique and special, but not odd or weird. The activities in this chapter focus on uniqueness. They attempt to help children recognize the ways they and others are different—from handprints to hair color to jobs—and also to see what similarities exist within those differences.

These activities should help children's self-image by helping them describe themselves in a variety of ways. It should support self-esteem by reinforcing positive evaluations of the diversity among people. Finally, it helps children begin to explore social identity and social justice issues by addressing issues of bias based on group differences.

Objectives

For Young Children
- To identify some ways people are different from each other.
- To identify some social groups to which they and others belong.
- To be able to describe themselves in simple terms to others.
- To learn some of the different combinations of members who make up families.
- To explore some of the types of jobs adults do.

For Early Elementary Children:
- To learn how differences between people are used as a basis for discrimination.
- To identify several social groups to which they and others belong and explore how those groups are viewed by society.
- To describe themselves in positive terms to others.
- To identify several types of families, including their own.
- To explore the tasks involved in a number of adult jobs.

For Later Elementary Children:
- To learn to say positive things about themselves without bragging.
- To experience some of the consequences of discrimination.
- To explore the balance between similarities and differences among people.
- To explore the social changes reflected in changing family forms.
- To identify some characteristics of jobs in which they have some interest.

For All Children:
- To view differences among people without value judgments.
- To explore the concept of discrimination.
- To build positive self-concepts.
- To identify some ways they may have an impact on the reduction of discrimination in their worlds.

Who I Am Book

You Will Need:

- paper
- glue
- crayons or markers
- photos of you and your friends or family
- stapler or paper punch and string

What To Do:

1. Collect some photos of you and your friends and family. Make sure they are photos you may keep. Or draw pictures that tell about you. Use the photos or pictures to tell a story about you. Glue one or two photos or pictures on a page. Be sure to say what is special about you.

2. Make a book. Fasten the pages together with the stapler or paper punch and string. Write (or have a grown-up write) your story to go with the pictures.

Let's Talk About It:

What does your story say about you? Are there ways that you are different from every other person? Are there ways that you are like every other person? Can someone reading your story pick out those things?

How does it feel to talk about how you are special? How is that different from bragging?

Who are the people you like to be with? Did you include them in your book? How are they like you and how are they different from you? How are they like or different from each other?

Other Things To Do:

Get to know someone new in your church or school. It might be someone that you think is very different from yourself. Find out what things that person likes to do. What does he or she think is interesting and important?

A Make the shape of a person on a large piece of paper. Cut pictures out of magazines or draw pictures that remind you of you. Glue them inside the person shape. What does this collage say about who you are?

Handprinting

You Will Need:
- ink pad OR thin fingerpaint
- a large sheet of paper
- magnifying glass

What To Do:
1. Spread fingerpaint out on a table or pan. Then press your hand on it. Or press your hand on an ink pad.

2. Put your hand on the paper to make a hand-print. Write your name beside your print. Have your friends or family make their handprints, too.

3. Use the magnifying glass. See the differences between the handprints. No two are alike!

Let's Talk About It:
How are the handprints different? What are the different sizes, shapes, and patterns?
What other differences are there in the way people look? Look at hair, eyes, noses, and ears. Look at clothes, glasses, and the way people walk. Can you tell what kind of person someone is by the way they look?

Other Things To Do:
Use fingerprints or footprints for the project.
Use acrylic paint for the project and make finger, hand, or footprints on cloth. Make T-shirts, tablecloths, or potholders. The acrylic paint will not wash out after it dries.
*A*Make "silhouette" or "shadow" drawings of your family members, friends, or class. Cut out the drawings. What is different in the drawings? Can you recognize the different people from their shadows?
Practice "strength bombardment." Have a time when your class or your family tells each other what is special about them. Maybe at suppertime each person can take a turn telling each other family member what is special about him or her. Or you can thank each person for doing something kind that day.

Touch Game

You Will Need:

- one or more families or lots of friends
- a leader

What To Do:

1. The leader should think of things for all the other people to look for. Some things to look for are "someone with a red shirt," "someone with black hair," or "someone with glasses." Or think of things that will make people ask questions, like "someone who is six years old" or "someone who hates lima beans."

2. Each person should find someone like that and gently touch that person.

3. Each time a new direction is given, look for whatever is called. Sometimes a person may get touched by lots of people! Remember to be respectful and kind to each person!

Let's Talk About It:

How do people look different from each other? How else are people different?

All people should be treated with care and respect. This is true even if they look or dress differently than you do, whether they are old or young, and no matter what they believe in. Does that always happen? Why not?

What "groups" do you belong to? Think about race, sex, religion, ethnic background, handicaps, and other groups. What feels good about being in those groups? What feels sad?

Other Things To Do:

A Plan a day or two when the people in half of your class or family are chosen as the ones to get extra privileges, such as more snack and special activities. The "privileged half" might be those wearing blue and red, or those with brown eyes, or some other group. Then switch and do similar things with the other half. How does it feel to be one of the people getting more? How does it feel to get less? Is it fair? Talk about discrimination and how people have experienced it.

Find out more about your race, sex, religion, or other group and how it is special. What important things have people in your group done? Talk with your family, community leaders, and others. Share what you find out with other people and listen as they share with you.

Learn about people from a social group that is different from yours. Talk with someone from that group. What things are important to him or her? Look up books, records or tapes, and other information in the library.

All Kinds of Families

You Will Need:
- crayons or markers
- paper

What To Do:

1. Think about the people who are a part of your family. It may be the people who live with you. It may include other family members that live farther away, too.

2. Draw a picture of your family. You may want to make your picture of a "family tree," with all of your family members as branches. Share your picture with your family and friends.

Let's Talk About It:

Who did you include in your family? How are these people important in your life? How does it feel to be a part of your family? When is it happy? When is it sad?

How are families different from each other? Do you know other children whose families are different from yours?

Other Things To Do:

Do this project with friends. Put all of your pictures together in a book about all kinds of families.

Talk to people with different kinds of families—someone with a new baby, someone who lives alone, or someone with an adopted family member. How do they feel about their families?

Make notes for your family. Tell them how much you love them and how they are special to you.

Make a picture of the kind of family you would like to live in when you grow up.

All Kinds of Jobs

You Will Need:
- paper • crayons or markers • glue
  - pictures of people doing
    different jobs

What To Do:

1. Think about all the different people you meet during the day. Think of the different jobs they do, like teacher, mail carrier, computer programmer, or homemaker. What other kinds of jobs are there?

2. Draw pictures of different jobs or cut them out of magazines. Glue your pictures on a large piece of paper to make a poster. Or glue them on smaller pieces of paper and staple them together to make a book about jobs.

Let's Talk About It:

Why do people work?

What jobs do your parents do? Where do they go? What do they do at work? Do they use special tools or wear special clothes?

What jobs do you think would be interesting? Do you think there are some jobs that are just for boys or men or just for girls or women? Why or why not?

How would it feel to be unemployed—to not have a job when you need one? How would it feel to be in that family?

Are there jobs that are important that do not earn money? Think about volunteer work or taking care of a home and family.

Other Things To Do:

Talk with your friends about what jobs their parents do. Where do they go? What do they do at work? Do they use special tools or wear special clothes?

A Visit the places where your parents or grandparents work. Or maybe you could visit your friends' parents. Find out what they do. Find out how they chose their jobs. Ask lots of questions!

O Talk with a woman who is doing a job that men usually do (like truck driver, doctor, or mayor). Or talk to a man who is doing a job that women usually do (like nurse, child care provider, or secretary). Ask how they chose their jobs. Ask about the problems they have with doing their jobs.

5

People Who Need People

Background information:

Understanding the balance between similarities and differences in people—the fact that all people are unique but share various needs, emotions, and environments—is a key to both positive self-concept and respect for others. After focusing on uniqueness and differences in chapter 4, this chapter is concerned with similarities among people, specifically feelings that everyone has in common, but which also are unique to individuals in unique situations.

The primary theme in this chapter is how people communicate their feelings with others. Communication has been defined as "shared knowledge." It is a key to bridging gaps between people. Communication of feelings is perhaps the most important type of communication and one of the more difficult types. Positive methods of communicating negative feelings is one of the most powerful tools to give children to avoid misbehavior and aggressive or violent actions. Children need to know that their feelings are accepted when they express those feelings in positive ways. Adults should assure children that all feelings are okay, but that positive communication of feelings is important.

Activities begin with practicing the identification of feelings by observing others. The face is probably the most expressive part of the body, but body language and the interaction of body and words also are covered here. Another aspect of communication covered here is the need for feedback from the listener.

Children who can communicate their feelings, in addition to being less likely to resort to violence to express themselves, may feel more competent and confident. Others will understand them better. They will have some important tools for conflict management. Adults need to be open to the children's attempts to communicate and need to share their own feelings in return.

Objectives

For Young Children:
- To label major categories of emotions.
- To recognize facial expressions of several emotions.
- To understand the basic concept of body language.
- To use pantomime to express themselves to others.

For Early Elementary Children:

- To identify some variations of major categories of emotions.
- To explore the ambiguity of some communication.
- To identify the components of communication; e.g., facial expression, body language, and words.
- To consider the impact of certain handicaps on communication.

For Later Elementary Children:

- To polish their skills in communicating with facial expression, body language, and words.
- To identify some fine distinctions among emotions.
- To learn to cooperate with others in communication.
- To learn the importance of effective communication in building trust.

For All Children:

- To develop a positive attitude toward emotions and learn positive ways to express them.
- To use puppets as a nonthreatening and fun means of communicating.

Faces Game

You Will Need:
- faces!

What To Do:

1. Make a list of different feelings that people have.

2. Make your face show the different feelings.

3. Think of other ways people show how they feel. Act out those other body movements to show different feelings. Take turns acting out a feeling while the others guess what it is.

Let's Talk About It:
How can you know how people feel by looking at their faces? Do you ever think you know how someone feels by looking at the face, and then find out you are wrong?

What other parts of bodies help to show what people are feeling?

How many different kinds of happy feelings can you think of? How do people show those different feelings? How many different kinds of sad, scared, and angry feelings can you think of?

Other Things To Do:
Notice how people show feelings during the day. Make a list of the feelings you see and how people show them. Notice ways that make other people feel good. Watch for ways of showing feelings that hurt another person. How can people hurt others by showing happy feelings, angry feelings, or sad feelings?

Think of a color. Take turns with your family or friends thinking of what feelings that color makes you think of. Think of other colors and the feelings you think of.

Have a friend think of a feeling. Close your eyes. Have your friend say a nursery rhyme using that feeling. Guess what the feeling is. Take turns closing your eyes and guessing. Can you tell how someone feels without looking?

Feelings Book

You Will Need:
- paper
- glue
- crayons or markers
- scissors
- people pictures showing different feelings

What To Do:

1. Look for pictures in magazines that show different feelings and cut them out. Or draw your own pictures.

2. Make a page for each feeling you found in the pictures. Label the pages. Write "Happy is." and other feelings at the top or bottom of each page. Glue pictures on each page that show that feeling.

3. Put the pages together into a book.

Let's Talk About It:
How did you decide which picture showed which feeling?
Who has feelings?
How does it feel to be able to tell someone about your feelings?

Other Things To Do:
Think about times when you have felt happy, sad, angry, jealous, or whatever. Write down the stories of what happened and how you felt. Or have an adult write the stories for you. Make a book of stories about feelings.

A Take photos of people showing different kinds of feelings. Make a photo book of feelings.

Listen to different kinds of music and tell whether the music makes you feel happy, sad, angry, scared, or other kinds of feelings.

Sock Puppets

You Will Need:

- socks (light-colored socks are good for drawing faces)

- colored markers
  or
  buttons and felt, scissors
  needle and thread or glue

What To Do:

1. Draw a face on the toe end of the sock. Or use buttons or pieces of felt and yarn to make the face and hair. Sew the pieces on or glue them.

2. Make your puppet talk. Put your hand in the sock and move your fingers or move your whole hand.

3. Talk about the puppet's feelings. Is the puppet happy? Sad? Angry? Scared? Act out stories with your puppets that show feelings.

Let's Talk About It:

Talk about times that you felt different ways. When did you feel sad, scared, happy, or surprised? What happened? Who were the people who were there with you? Did your feelings change? How can you have puppets act out those stories?

Is it easier to talk about feelings with the puppets than it is to talk about your own feelings? Why do you think that is?

How do you show feelings with puppets?

Other Things To Do:

Work on and practice one or two stories that you would like to share as a "puppet show" with your family, some friends, younger children, or another class. Be sure to include different kinds of feelings in your show.

Tape record music to add to a puppet show.

O Make different kinds of puppets. You may want to try a marionette—a puppet with strings.

A Make a puppet theater.

Communication

You Will Need:
- family or friends

What To Do:
1. Think about something you did yesterday or today. It could be playing a game, taking a bath, or walking the dog.

2. Take turns with your family or friends trying to tell each other what you did without using words. Use your hands, face, arms, legs, or anything you need, but do not use your voice.

Body Talk

No Peeking!

You Will Need:
- one friend or more
- building blocks

(if younger children try this, pair them with an adult)

What To Do:
1. Sit on the floor with your back against your friend's back. Pick out two, three, or four blocks. Give your partner blocks that are the same size, shape, and color.

2. Make a tower with your blocks on the floor in front of you. Tell your partner how to make the same tower. No peeking!

3. Look to see if your partner's tower looks like yours. Then let your partner make a tower and tell you how to make it.

Let's Talk About It:

How did it feel to use just your body or just words to tell someone something?

Did you understand each other? What was easy and what was hard to communicate?

How do people use words and bodies together to tell people their ideas?

What are some ways that people tell others something without speaking? How do people use their bodies or faces to show what they mean?

How hard would it be to understand other people if you could not see? How important is it to look at someone who is talking to you?

Why do all people need to communicate? What would it be like if you could not communicate at all?

How does it feel when you hear or see another language that you do not understand?

Other Things To Do:

Learn some words in another language. Use books, records, or tapes, or talk with someone who can speak that language. You might want to start by learning some songs, phrases, counting, or words for things.

Spend some time with a baby. Watch the baby's "body talk." Try to figure out what he or she needs and what will make your little friend happy.

Learn some words or sentences in sign language. Maybe you could learn to "sign" with a song you like.

⑥
Things Everyone Needs

Background information:
This chapter builds further on the concept in the previous chapter of similarities among people. In addition to having emotions in common, another similarity among people involves basic life needs. All people need food, clothes, and shelter, and these are items that children can understand and areas in which they can have an impact. These resources also represent some areas in which unequal distribution of wealth is evident among nations, geographic areas, and social groups.

Telling children they need to eat their broccoli because children are starving in Ethiopia is not a very effective way to build social consciousness. The activities in this chapter attempt to make the concepts of hunger and lack of clothing and housing more concrete. They also provide some ways that children can have an impact on people in need short of sticking their broccoli in an envelope and sending it across the ocean.

The awareness of food distribution issues begins with an understanding of good nutrition and of where foods on the table or in the grocery store originate. A feeling of satisfaction and control can come from the experiences of making soup and bread. A sense of personal responsibility in cutting down on food waste and eating healthy foods is another contribution toward dealing with hunger in the world. Although fasting and experiencing hunger are strategies used by teens and adults in building hunger awareness, this method is inappropriate for young children. Rather than feeling guilty about having good food, children should learn that personal responsibility is an important contribution.

Concerning clothing issues, the recycling project addresses both waste and need issues. The shelter project makes children aware of different sizes and types of housing and introduces the concept of homelessness.

Objectives

For Young Children:
- To learn that bread is made and not grown.
- To become aware of food waste and their personal contribution to it.
- To learn some reasons for passing used clothing on to others.
- To explore issues of space in housing.

For Early Elementary Children:

- To learn some basic cooking techniques.
- To apply some basic nutrition information to food preparation.
- To explore the concept of unequal distribution of resources.
- To assist in the sharing of clothing resources with people in need.
- To think about the idea of personal space.

For Later Elementary Children:

- To plan and carry out a cooking project.
- To explore the impact of various food processing methods on nutritional food quality.
- To define the difference between abundance and need and to place themselves along that continuum.
- To explore ways to share wealth with people in need.

For All Children:

- To cook food that can be shared by the family and others.
- To learn simple techniques of becoming a responsible consumer of food and clothing.
- To build bridges with people in need in the community and in the world.
- To make contact with agencies and organizations which distribute resources to people in need.

A Back to Basics—Breadmaking

You Will Need:

- a large bowl
- a big spoon
- a pan
- a clean cloth
- measuring cups and spoons
- 2 bread pans
- a warm place

Ingredients:
8 cups whole wheat flour (or 4 c. white and 4 c. whole wheat)
2 packages dry yeast
3 cups water
1/2 cup honey
2 tablespoons oil (plus a little more)

What To Do:

1. Stir 3 cups of flour and the yeast together in the bowl.

2. Mix the water, honey, and 2 T. oil in the pan. Heat it on the stove until warm (not hot).

3. Pour the warm liquid over the flour and yeast mixture.

4. Beat 300 times.

5. Stir in the rest of the flour.

6. Knead (push and squeeze it hard with your hands) for 5 minutes. Wash and oil the bowl.

7. Put the dough in the bowl and let it rise in a warm place. Let it rise until it is twice as big as it was to start.

8. Punch the dough down, divide it into two halves, and form loaves.

9. Put the two loaves in the bread pans, cover them with the cloth, and let them rise for 45 minutes.

10. Bake the bread at 375 degrees for 45 minutes. Eat!

Let's Talk About It:

What makes the bread rise? What would it be like to bake the bread without letting it rise?

Was it a lot of work to knead the bread?

How does this bread taste different from store-bought bread? Does bread you make yourself taste better than bread you just buy at the store?

What would it be like if you had to make all of your own bread?

Other Things To Do:

A Try making different kinds of bread from different cultures and places in the world.

A Make other basic, simple foods to eat. Many people of the world live on rice, beans, and bread. What would it be like to live on that diet?

Garden Soup

You Will Need:
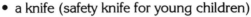
- a large pot
- fresh garden vegetables
- cutting board
- a wooden spoon
- water, soup stock, or tomato juice
- salt and pepper
- a knife (safety knife for young children)

What to Do:
1. Choose some fresh vegetables from the store or from your garden.

2. *A* Cut up the vegetables into chunks.

3. Put your chunky vegetables and some water, stock, or tomato juice in a pot. Add salt and pepper, if you like.

4. *A* Cook for one or two hours. Check and stir now and then. Eat!

Let's Talk About It:
How is eating food that you grow yourself different from eating grocery store food?
Why are vegetables fresh from the garden good for your body?

Other Things To Do:
A Visit a local food cooperative. How is the food there different? Are the packages different? Do you see these kinds of foods on television commercials? Why or why not?

Learn about the food groups—dairy, meat (including other protein foods and combinations), fruits and vegetables, and bread and cereals. What things are good for bodies? Which are not so good? What do people mean when they talk about "junk food?"

Make "stone soup" with your friends. Have each friend bring one vegetable or something else to put in the soup. Read the story *Stone Soup*. Talk about how it feels to work together to make something special.

Hungry People

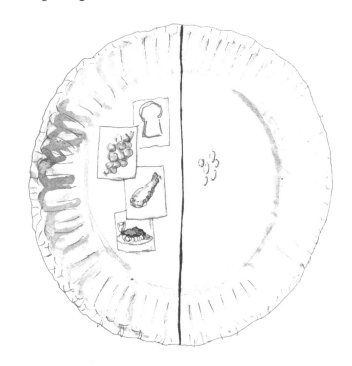

You Will Need:

- a paper plate

- magazines with pictures of food

- scissors   • glue

- a few grains of rice

- crayon

What To Do:
1. Cut out pictures of lots of different kinds of colorful foods that you like to eat. Draw a line down the middle of your plate.

2. On one side glue pictures of all the different foods you like to eat. On the other side glue two or three grains of rice.

Let's Talk About It:
What would it feel like to have the rice side as your dinner plate?
Can you think of ways to share what you have with others?
How does it feel to know that many people are really hungry while others have food that they throw away?
Why do you think some people have lots of food and other people have very little?

Other Things To Do:
Try to waste less food. Serve yourself only as much as you can eat at mealtime. Measure the waste from each meal. See if you can have no waste at all after some meals.
A Have a food (canned goods) collection project. Give the food to a local "food bank" for people who do not have enough to eat.
A Raise money (maybe with a recycling project) to buy a healthy animal to send to a community in need. Write to:
Heifer Project International
P.O. Box 808
Little Rock, Arkansas 72203

Clothes Recycling Project

You Will Need:
- boxes   • markers   • clothes
    • a place to collect the clothes

What To Do:
1. Ask the people from your family, neighborhood, school, or church to bring clothing to the collection space for giving away. They can be clothes that the family cannot wear anymore or clothes that they want to give to someone who needs them. The clothes should be clean and in good shape.

2. Sort the clothes into boxes, one box for grown-ups, one for children. You can label the boxes with pictures or words. You may know of a particular family that needs and would like clothing. Pick out those sizes that are needed.

3. *A* Call the local Goodwill, Salvation Army, Church World Service, or similar place and ask about how you could give them the clothes. Sometimes there are other groups in your community that are collecting clothing for people who need it. You could check with those groups also.

Let's Talk About It:
> How many clothes do you think you need for yourself? How many do you have in your closet or dresser at home?
> How is it helpful to wear hand-me-downs or second-hand clothes?
> How can you help when there are children who need clothes? Why should clothes that you give away be in good shape?

Other Things To Do:
> *O* Learn to fix your own clothes when they get torn or a button falls off.
> *A* Look up books in the library about what different kinds of clothes are needed or worn in different places of the world. How do people get or make their clothes? What kinds of material do they use? Do they use machines or make clothing by hand?
> *A* Think of other clothing projects, such as a mitten tree at Christmas or Hanukkah for children in colder places. Ask everyone in your family, church, or school to give a pair of mittens to decorate a tree. Then give the mittens to a school or group that can offer them to children who need them.

Shelter For All

You Will Need:
- a large piece of paper
- a small piece of paper
- crayons or markers
- department store catalogue and glue, if you want

What To Do:
1. Draw a picture of your home on the large piece of paper. Make the different rooms in your home. Add furniture and other things that are in the rooms. Draw and color or cut and paste pictures from the catalogue. Draw the people in your family, too.

2. Now draw a house with only one room on the small piece of paper. Add furniture and your family to this picture, too.

Let's Talk About It:
How much could you fit in your second picture? Was it crowded for the furniture and the family?

What would it be like to have only one room for your furniture and other things and for your family? What would it be like to have no home at all? How would it feel in the summer? How would it feel in the winter?

Do you have a special place just for you in your house? How much space do you need?

Other Things To Do:
Find out if there are people in your community who are homeless. Think of ways you could help by sharing food, clothing, or writing a letter to your newspaper or mayor about the homeless.

A Visit a shelter for the homeless and take food or clothing to share.

Find out if there is a *Habitat for Humanity* group in your community. Talk with them about how they build homes. Ask if there is anything that children can do to help.

Learn about different kinds of homes in which people live and have lived. Learn about other cultures and other historical eras.

O Make a model of your home or other types of homes with boxes, sticks, cloth, clay, and other materials.

7
People All Over the World

Background information:

Boundaries, borders, and separations among groups of people are some of the major contributors to conflict and strife among people. The more narrowly a person defines his or her "home," "family," or other group deserving of loyalty, the more conflict is created. The concept of a world family is difficult for young children to truly grasp, however. They may have a hard time just understanding the idea of "neighbors." But most children readily accept the value of others, so they may make up for the cognitive immaturity with emotional enthusiasm.

The idea that all people are part of the world family is based on similarities among people, but those similarities are balanced with the differences in culture and daily life among countries and subcultures. Learning to appreciate, understand, and respect those differences is important for young peacemakers. Otherwise they may find themselves facing fear, jealousy, or ridicule of those who are different from themselves.

Young children cannot understand the concepts of nations, ethnic groups, or cultural heritage in an abstract way, but they can identify with many of the ways those concepts are translated into everyday life. Learning about the foods, houses, games, clothing, and schools in other parts of the world is fascinating to most children and will help to make the world seem smaller and more understandable. Actually meeting people from those places is another way to make abstract concepts concrete. In addition, international contact will make it difficult for those children to build an "image of the enemy"—a central part of a country's warmaking effort—if they know a kind and caring person from the targeted country.

Objectives

For Young Children:
- To learn that daily life is different in different countries.
- To learn that people in different parts of the world speak different langauges, but that they talk about many of the same things.
- To learn what maps and globes are used for.

For Early Elementary Children:
- To identify some traditions and practices used by people in one or two other countries.
- To learn a few words or a song in another language.
- To be able to find a few places on a map or globe.

For Later Elementary Children:
- To explore how some cultural practices are related to weather, geography, history, and so on.
- To describe the difference between allegiance to one country vs. allegiance to the world.
- To identify several practices or artifacts by the country or culture of origin.

For All Children:
- To develop a relationship with someone from another country.
- To have fun with games, stories, and toys from other cultures.
- To develop an appreciation and respectful curiosity about cultures different from their own.

World Family Collage

You Will Need:

- large paper or cardboard
- magazines with pictures of people from around the world (like *National Geographic*)
- glue
- crayons or markers
- scissors

What To Do:

1. Cut out pictures of people from all over the world. Include many different types of people doing many different things.

2. Think of a name for your collage. Some ideas are "Hands Across the World," "We Are the World," or "My World Family." With big letters, write the words on your paper or cardboard.

3. Glue people pictures all over the paper or cardboard, leaving the words showing.

4. Find a good place for sharing your collage with others.

Let's Talk About It:

How do the people from different countries look different? Can you tell what country people are from by looking at their faces? Can you tell by looking at their clothes?

Do all of the people look alike in some ways?

What kinds of things do people do all over the world?

Other Things To Do:

Make a poster with pictures of just babies from around the world, another with just children, one with mothers, one with fathers, and/or one with old people.

Read stories of people and children from other countries. Think about how their lives are similar and different from yours.

A Talk with a family that has adopted a child from another country or has had an exchange student. Ask in what ways the children or teens were just like kids from this country. Ask in what ways they were different.

Friends From Far Away

You Will Need:
- one or more guests from another country or culture
(it may be someone from your neighborhood, church, or school)

What To Do:
1. Invite your guests to come and share a meal or "tea" with your family, friends, or class. Ask them to share a recipe you could try.

2. Ask if they have some things they could show you from their country or culture. These could include clothes, musical instruments, toys, art or crafts, money, pictures or slides.

3. Think of questions you might ask your guest. Some things you might like to know about could be homes, schools, food and clothing, games children play, how the countryside looks, how cities or villages look, holidays and festivals, songs and music, religious traditions and rituals, and animals.

4. Your guests might share some of these things with you:

   tell a poem or story in their language;
   sing a children's song;
   teach a children's game or dance; or
   tell stories of their childhood.

Let's Talk About It:
What did you like most about your guests' visit? What things have you learned from the visit? In what ways did their lives in their country seem most like yours? In what ways did they seem most different?
Is there anything that was mentioned during the visit that you would like to learn more about?

Other Things To Do:
O Look at a globe. Find out where you live and where your guests came from. What else can you find on the globe?
Use ideas that came up during the visit. Plan some activities that interest you. You might make a map of the country, learn some of your guests' language, do a cooking project, or plan a festival or celebration.
A Go to the library to learn more about the country or culture of your guests.
A Invite one or more guests from a different country to visit later.

Folk Stories From Many Lands

You Will Need:

- a library

What To Do:

1. Find the folk stories and folktales section of the children's area of your library.

2. Choose a book to read. Read the story. Look at the pictures if there are any. Think about what the story means and what ideas it shares. Look for ideas about life and death; being rich or poor; justice and injustice; and love, magic, and nature.

Let's Talk About It:

What was the story about? In what country did the story take place?
What things did you learn from the story? What did you learn about the country?
How did the story make you feel? Was it funny, sad, or happy?
Did the story tell about life and death? What did it have to say? Did it tell about being rich or poor, justice and injustice, or love, magic, and nature?

Other Things To Do:

Read more folk stories and folktales from other countries.
Choose a story to act out. Think about what people or animals you will need. What happens first? What happens next? Do you want to make costumes? What else will you need? Make a plan and then act out the story for your family or friends.
Make a poster showing and telling about your favorite folktale. Or make a book telling the story with pictures that you draw.
Make up your own folktale from a funny, sad, or happy experience you have had or thought of.

O World Pledge Poster

You Will Need:
- large paper
- magazines with pictures of people, plants, animals, and other living things
- crayons or markers
- scissors
- glue

The World Pledge
"I pledge allegiance to the world,
To cherish every living thing,
To care for earth and sea and air,
With peace and freedom everywhere."
Lillian Genser

What To Do:
1. Write the World Pledge on your paper. Or have someone older write it for you.

2. Cut out pictures of living things. Make your own drawings, too, of people, plants, and animals. Use the pictures to decorate your poster.

Let's Talk About It:
What do the words and phrases in the pledge mean? (Look up these words from the pledge in the dictionary: pledge, allegiance, cherish, peace, and freedom.)
How is it different from pledging allegiance to one flag or country?

Other Things To Do:
Share the pledge with others. Display your poster in a public place.
Think of how you would say the pledge using your own words. Make a poster with your words.
Learn how to say the pledge with sign language.
Make a separate picture or poster for each line of the pledge. Use pictures that go with each line to decorate the posters.
Find other pledges, like the *Pledge of Allegiance to the Flag*. Try to find pledges from other countries. Look up the words in those pledges. Do they use different words? How else are they different?

Resource List

Understanding People

Books:

Felker, Donald W. *Building Positive Self-Concepts.* Minneapolis: Burgess, 1974.

Longacre, Doris Janzen. *Living More With Less.* Scottdale: Herald Press, 1980.

Longacre, Doris Janzen. *More With Less Cookbook.* Scottdale: Herald Press, 1977.

McGinnis, Kathleen and James. *Parenting for Peace and Justice.* Maryknoll, NY: Orbis Books, 1981.

McNeill and others. *Cultural Awareness for Young Children* (Asian, Black, Cowboy, Eskimo, Mexican, Native American cultures). The Learning Tree, 9998 Ferguson Rd., Dallas, TX 75228.

Prutzman, P., Burger, M. L., Bodenhamer, G., and Stern, L. *The Friendly Classroom for a Small Planet.* Wayne, NJ: Avery Publishing Group, 1978.

Saracho and Spodek. *Understanding the Multicultural Experience in Early Childhood Education.* Washington, DC: National Association for the Education of Young Children, 1983.

Wanamaker, Nancy. *More Than Graham Crackers: Nutrition Education and Food Preparation with Young Children.* Washington, DC: National Association for the Education of Young Children, 1979.

Wolf, Dennie Palmer (Ed.) *Connecting: Friendship in the Lives of Young Children and Their Teachers.* Redmond, Washington: Exchange Press, 1986.

Zander, Janet. *World Food Day: Curriculum/Grades K–3.* Office on Global Education, Church World Service, 2115 N. Charles St., Baltimore, MD 21218, 1986.

Children's Books:

Aliki. *The Story of Johnny Appleseed.*

Andersen, Hans Christian. *The Little Match Girl* and *The Ugly Duckling.*

Burns, Marilyn. *I Am Not a Short Adult! Getting Good at Being a Kid.*

Byars, Betsy. *Go and Hush the Baby.*

O Davidson, Margaret. *Helen Keller.*

Drescher, Joan. *Your Family, My Family.*

Fassler, Joan. *Howie Helps Himself.*

Flournoy, Valerie. *The Patchwork Quilt.*

Herriot, James. *Moses the Kitten.*

Heine, Helme. *Friends.*

Hill, Elizabeth Starr. *Evan's Corner.*

Jenkins. *Kinder Krunchies: Healthy Snack Recipes for Children.* Distributed by Discovery Toys, Pleasant Hill, CA 94523.

Keats, Jack Ezra. *Peter's Chair* and *Whistle for Willie.*

Lasker, Joe. *He's My Brother.*

McGovern, Ann. *Stone Soup.*

Museum of Modern Art. *The Family of Man* and *The Family of Children.*

Schweitzer, B. B. *Amigo.*

Silverstein, Shel. *The Missing Piece.*

Spier, Peter. *People.*

Steig, William. *Amos and Boris.*

Udry. *What Mary Jo Shared.*

Viorst, Judith. *Alexander and the Terrible, Horrible, No Good Very Bad Day* and *The Tenth Good Thing About Barney.*

Yashima, Taro. *The Crow Boy.*

Folktales:

Aardema, Verna. *Bringing the Rain to Kapiti Plain* (Africa) and *Why Mosquitos Buzz in People's Ears* (West Africa).

Baylor Byrd. *A God on Every Mountaintop: Stories of the Southwest Indian Sacred Mountains.*

De Paola, Tomie. *The Mysterious Giant of Barletta* (Italy).

Fardjam, Farida. *The Crystal Flower and the Sun* (Persia).

McDermott, Beverly Brodsky. *Sedna, An Eskimo Myth.*

McDermott, Gerald. *Arrow to the Sun* (Pueblo)

Miles, Mishka. *Annie and the Old One* (Navajo)

Otsuka, Yuzo. *Suho and the White Horse: A Legend of Mongolia.*

Rose, Ann. *Akimba and the Magic Cow* (Africa).

Wolkstein, Diane. *The Banza* (Haiti).

Organizations:

Center for Teaching About Peace and War
Wayne State University
Detroit, MI 48202

Christian Rural Overseas Program (CROP)
28606 Phillips Street, Elkhart, IN 46515

Council on Interracial Books for Children
1841 Broadway, New York, NY 10023

Global Food Crisis
Church of the Brethren
1451 Dundee Avenue, Elgin, IL 60120

Gryphon House
3706 Otis Street-P.O. Box 275
Mt. Rainier, MD 20712
1-800-638-0928
  Publishers and distributor of children's books. Ask for catalogues and resource lists.

Heifer Project International
P.O. Box 808
Little Rock, Arkansas 72203

Teachers College Press
Teachers College
Columbia University
New York, NY 10027
  Publisher of resource books for teachers. Ask for catalogue— Early Childhood Education Series.

UNICEF
331 East 38th Street
New York, NY 10016

Section III
Making Peace

Be a Friend

Background information:

It takes skill to be a friend. Children must be willing to make acquaintance with new people, to use effective strategies for becoming friends, and to learn how to communicate and work through conflicts. This chapter deals with strategies for meeting new people and establishing friendships in addition to methods for expressing concern and caring to friends who need support.

Many children are uncomfortable in unfamiliar settings and with unfamiliar people. At the same time that peer judgments and support become very important in middle childhood, children still are developing social skills, especially involving meeting new people. Social skills, including the ability to make and keep friends, are central to peacemaking.

A group with which it may be even harder for children to interact than unfamiliar children is senior citizens. Because of prevalence of age segregation in modern society, many children will have had limited opportunities to make friends with elderly individuals. Such a friendship is likely to benefit both the child and the older person. Children will gain knowledge of a different point in history, will be able to observe the aging process, and may be able to serve an important helping role for another person. The elder will have the opportunity to interact with a lively, energetic, creative young person who probably will not take the aging process too seriously, as adults may be prone to do.

Finally, some ideas are presented to help young people use their creativity to express caring and concern to those who need support. Friends who are sick or far away and people who are lonely or in prison can be reached and cared for, even if the children cannot be with them.

Objectives

For Young Children:
- To identify the feelings of a person when effective and noneffective strategies for friendship-making are used.
- To identify some of the needs and abilities of the elderly.
- To make a greeting card and mail it.

For Early Elementary Children:
- To identify one or two effective strategies for making a new friend.
- To plan at least one appropriate activity for themselves and an elderly person.
- To prepare an appropriate greeting card for someone in need of support.
- To identify one or two appropriate activities for a sick or lonely child.

For Later Elementary Children:
- To explain why effective stategies for making new friends work and why ineffective strategies do not.
- To plan and carry out an ongoing "adoptive relationship" with an elderly person.
- To prepare appropriate greetings for at least three different occasions and describe their appropriateness.
- To plan a package of appropriate and balanced activities for a sick or lonely child.

For All Children:
- To plan strategies for meeting new people.
- To build a positive relationship with an elderly person and to develop a positive view of aging.
- To use their creativity to express concern and caring to another individual.
- To identify people in need of support.

Making New Friends

You Will Need:

- 4 pieces of paper numbered 1,2,3, and 4
- crayons or markers OR pictures of people looking happy, sad, scared, and angry and glue

What To Do:

1. Pretend you are new in a class or group. You do not know anyone else. Pretend one of the kids sneaked up behind you and pulled your hair, laughed, and ran away. Draw or glue a picture on paper #1 that shows how you would feel if that happened to you.

2. Pretend you heard one of the kids say to another, "I think that new kid is funny-looking. Let's just go play by ourselves." Draw or glue a picture on paper #2 that shows how you would feel.

3. Pretend one of the kids walked up to you and said, "Hi. My name is Pat. Do you want to play ball with me?" Draw or glue a picture on paper #3 that would show how you would feel.

4. Pretend you said hi to someone. That person just said "hi" and walked away to play with other kids. Draw or glue a picture on paper #4 that shows how you would feel.

Let's Talk About It:

Why did you choose the pictures you glued on your papers?

How does it feel to not have any friends around? How does it feel to make a new friend?

What is a good way to make a new person feel welcome in a group?

How can you tell if you want to be friends with new people? Can you tell by looking at them? Can you tell by talking with them?

Other Things To Do:

O Think of other actions that work and do not work when making a new friend.

O Make up a play about a new person joining a group. Show things that some people might say to or do for the new person. Show how the new person feels. Practice your play and act it out for your family or friends.

Think of someone you know who might need a new friend. Think of some ways you could make friends with that person. Try some of the ways.

A Adopt a Grandparent

You Will Need:

> • the name and address of a few senior citizens

What To Do:

1. Get the names of some older people who might need a young friend or two. A pastor, neighbor, or a senior center or nursing home might be able to supply you with names.

2. Choose a person to visit. Have a grown-up set up the visit for you.

3. Visit the person. Tell about yourself. Ask the person what he or she likes to do now. Ask about when he or she was your age.

4. If you like each other, you may want to ask the older person if he or she would like to be "adopted."

5. Call. Visit. Send cards, letters, or pictures you draw. Invite your new "grandparent" to visit you. Be in touch often.

Let's Talk About It:

Why are some older people lonely?

Is it hard to imagine that older people were once as little as you? What were things like back then? What did they like to do?

What are some things that older people might have trouble doing? Why? How could you help them? How can older people help you?

How is it different having a friend who is much older than you? What can you learn? What can you share?

Other Things To Do:

A group of children could "adopt" one or more "grandparents."

O Think of ways you can be helpful to an older neighbor or church member. Maybe you could rake leaves, shovel snow, or carry groceries.

O Find out what places and activities are available in your area for older people. Do they have interesting things to do? Are there people to take care of them if they need help?

If you have "real" grandparents or great-grandparents who live far away, send a picture or a letter. If they live close by, go for a visit.

Card Making

You Will Need:
- paper
- scissors
- crayons or markers
- pressed wildflowers or other nature things
- glue
- water
- white tissue paper
- paintbrush

What To Do:
1. Cut and fold paper to make a card in the size and shape you would like. Arrange pressed wildflowers or other nature things on the outside of the card.

2. Mix glue with water. Use a paintbrush to spread the watered-down glue over the flowers.

3. Cover the flowers with tissue paper. Let your art work dry. Write a message inside the card.

Let's Talk About It:
What are some times that people like to send cards? Are all the times happy? Why do people like to send cards?

How do you feel when you get a card from someone who cares?

How is a card that you make yourself different from a card you would buy at a store? How is the art work different? How are the messages inside the card different?

Other Things To Do:
Decorate the outside of your cards with other things. Try material scraps, small flower pictures, or colored tissue paper.

If you have a computer you can use, make a card with a computer graphics program.

Make different kinds of cards for different occasions.

A Care Fun-Pak

You Will Need:
- a container
- collage materials
- markers or caryons
- small activities or games for a child

What To Do:
1. Decorate the outside of your container or box with paper and collage materials.

2. Make the playdough (see below).

3. Make a paper notebook. Staple papers together for drawing. Decorate the outside of the notebook with your own drawing. Write the child's name on the outside.

4. Add other things to your fun-pak, such as markers or crayons, canning rings (for playdough activities), small books, or anything else you would like to give. Send or give the fun-pak to your friend!

Let's Talk About It:
How do people show others that they care about them?

Thing about a time when you were sick or lonely. How did you feel? How do you think your friend feels? What activities are good when you are just a little sick? What about when you are very sick? What activities are good when you are lonely?

Other Things To Do:
Think about someone you care about and would like to tell in a special way. Send that person some of your art work or crafts and photos that you think he or she would especially like.

O Make a fun-pak for someone who might be sick for a long time. Make special little packages to open every day for one or two weeks. Inside the packages put little activities, a poem, a photo, a tape, or some other surprise.

Playdough:

2 cups of flour	½ cup of salt
2 t. cream of tartar	2 T. oil
2 cups of water	food coloring

Mix dry ingredients. Add oil. Stir. Add water and food coloring. Stir and cook until it is playdough texture and pulls from the sides of the pan.

9

When Things Don't Work Out

Background information:

Having skills in solving problems helps children (and adults!) avoid resorting to violence when conflicts occur. A basic problem-solving model includes: 1) defining the problem; 2) brainstorming possible solutions; 3) evaluating alternatives; 4) making a plan; 5) carrying out the plan; and 6) evaluating the effectiveness of the solution. This chapter attempts to address each of these components.

An important part of this chapter is the creation of a "problem box" and a "response box." These boxes are important for the completion of the activities, but they also serve to help children build skills in the first two steps of the problem-solving model. Thinking of interpersonal problems and putting them in either picture or word form helps children with problem definition. Thinking of all possible alternatives for responding helps to increase their repertoire when a problem occurs. Rather than thinking only of crying or hitting, the "response box" should give them other choices to consider.

Other parts of the activities help children with the actual decisionmaking process by helping them consider and even act out possible results of using a variety of alternatives. Younger children will need to act out the alternatives in order to picture the consequences. As they get older and more experienced in problem-solving they may be able to imagine results in their heads.

Role playing is a difficult skill for very young children. It can be a lot of fun as they begin to develop the skill, however. It may be easier for younger ones to begin with puppets. Building role-playing skills will be an important step toward developing empathy and the ability to solve problems.

Objectives

For Young Children:
- To talk about different kinds of interpersonal problems.
- To learn that there are many possible solutions to interpersonal problems.
- To identify feelings of people who experience several types of problems and solutions.
- To practice a few alternative solutions to problems.
- To realize that their actions have an affect on the emotions of others.

Objectives

For Early Elementary Children:
- To use pictures or words to represent several types of interpersonal problems.
- To identify several possible responses to problems.
- To act out and judge the effectiveness and mutual support of several possible responses to problems.
- To begin to identify the steps of a problem-solving model.

For Later Elementary Children:
- To match interpersonal problems with possible solutions.
- To distinguish between effective and ineffective, supportive and nonsupportive responses to problems.
- To anticipate the reactions of others to possible responses to problems.
- To identify and carry out the steps of a problem-solving model.

For All Children:
- To experience the steps of a problem-solving model.
- To realize that others experience similar interpersonal problems to themselves.
- To create a "response box" with a number of possible actions from which to choose when a problem arises.
- To have fun considering alternative solutions to problems.

Problems, Problems, Problems

You Will Need:
- crayons, markers, paint and paintbrushes, or colored paper
- paper   • a shoe box

What To Do:

1. Think of different kinds of problems people sometimes have getting along with each other. Think of problems with friends or brothers and sisters (like not sharing things, hitting, or calling each other names). Think of problems between kids and parents or teachers (like kids not picking up their messes or grown-ups yelling at kids).

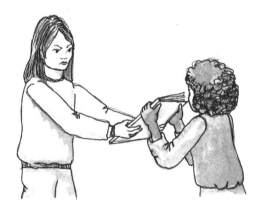 

2. Decide who is a part of each problem. Think of what kids are involved and what grown-ups are involved. (Young children may want to give each person a real or pretend name.)

3. Draw a picture of each problem. Maybe you will want to draw more than one picture to show what happens first, next, and last. Include all the people involved. Or write the problems down on pieces of paper. Then put the problems in a box.

Let's Talk About It:

Is it easier to think about problems between kids or problems between kids and adults?

Is it hard to put some problems into words or pictures?

Other Things To Do:

Count the number of times each of the problems happens for you.

Practice telling people about the problems you have.

Paper Plate Masks

You Will Need:
- paper plates
- glue or tape
- crayons, markers, paint and paintbrushes, or colored paper
- scissors
- popsicle sticks or tongue depressors

What To Do:
1. Take 5 paper plates. Draw, glue, or paint a face on each one. One face should be happy, one sad, one angry, one lonely, and one just okay—not happy or sad.

2. Cut holes for the eyes in each mask. Glue or tape a stick on the bottom to hold.

3. Get your problem box. Work together with a friend. Pick a problem out of the box.

4. Think about when you may have been in that situation. Choose which person you want to pretend to be. Pick out the mask that shows how that person might feel. Have your partner be someone else in the situation and pick out a mask, too.

5. Pick another problem out of the box and pick out masks again.

Let's Talk About It:
Do people ever seem happy when they are hurting someone else? Do you think it feels good to hurt someone?

Which kinds of problems make people sad? Which kinds make people angry? Which kinds make people feel lonely? Which kinds do not really matter to people?

Other Things To Do:
Pick a problem from the box. Try to think of all the reasons people might do those things.

Practice saying how you feel when you have a problem with your friends or with your parents.

Make more masks showing different kinds of feelings.

What Would Happen If

You Will Need:
- paper
- crayons or markers
- a shoe box
- yourself
- some friends
- your imagination
- your problem box (see p. 76)

What To Do:

1. Think of all the things people might do when they have a problem with friends or parents. Talking it over, hitting, making a deal, yelling, asking a grown-up for help, and crying are some things you might think of. Draw a picture of each response or write them down on pieces of paper.

2. Pick a problem out of the problem box. Ask "What would happen if . . . " and pick a response out of the response box.

3. Talk about what might happen if someone would do what the paper says. Think about whether it would help, make things worse, or if it just would not work at all. Think about other things to do. Write them down or draw a picture to add to your response box.

Let's Talk About It:

Is it hard to think of very many different things to do? Which responses would make everyone feel good? Which responses would make someone feel bad?

Which would work? Which would make the problem worse? What do you think would be the best way to solve the problem?

Other Things To Do:

The next time you have a problem with your friends or family, try some of the responses you thought might work. After you try a new response, decide if it worked. If it did not, try something else.

Set up a regular time each week to have a family or class meeting to talk about problems and work on solutions. Anybody should be allowed to bring up a problem to share. Write down your agenda before the meeting. Make sure everyone gets a chance to talk.

Role Playing

You Will Need:

- a partner or two
- puppets (if you want)
- your problem and response boxes (see pp. 76, 78)

What To Do:

1. Pick a problem from the problem box. Or think of another problem that comes up between people in your family or among your friends.

2. Think about these things: Who is involved in this problem? What happens first? What happens next?

3. Let each person or puppet be one of the people in the problem. Each person should take a minute to think about the person they are pretending to be and what he or she is like.

4. Choose a response from the response box and act out the story of the problem. Then choose a different response and act out the story again. Or let your group or family talk about what the solutions could be.

Let's Talk About It:

How did it feel to play the person you pretended to be?

What was easy about acting out the story? What was hard? If you played more than one part, which one was easier? Why?

Did acting out the problem help you think differently about it? Why?

Other Things To Do:

Trade places and pretend to be someone else.

Practice some stories to act out for your family or another class. Try many different responses to a problem. Talk about which responses worked best and why.

Think about a real problem you have had. Ask a friend to help you roleplay. Have your friend pretend to be you. You pretend to be the person you have the problem with. See how it feels to be the other person. Can you think of something new to do?

Problem Solving Book

You Will Need:
- paper
- crayons or markers
- your problem and response boxes
- a paper punch
- paper fasteners, string, or a loose leaf notebook

What To Do:
1. Make the paper into a book. Pick a problem from the problem box. Or think of a new problem. Draw a picture of the problem on one page.

2. On the next page draw a line down the middle from the top to the bottom. On one side draw a happy face. On the other side draw an unhappy face.

3. Pick a response from the response box or think of other responses. Decide whether each response would make people feel good or bad. Draw a picture or write each response on the side of the page where you think it belongs.

4. Pick new problems and add new pages. Make a cover for your problem book.

Let's Talk About It:
Are there some responses that make some people feel good and others feel bad? Where can you put those responses in your book? What responses can you think of that will make everyone feel good?

Does this book help you decide what to do about problems? Does writing ideas on paper help?

Did you have trouble thinking of any responses at all for some of the problems? How can you use your imagination to think of some ideas?

Other Things To Do:
Write stories that tell about a problem and how it was solved. Put your stories or stories from your friends into a book.

When real problems happen during your day, add them to your book. Use the book to help you decide what to do.

10
Be a Peace Hero

Background information:

This chapter is a young person's introduction to personal peace activism. Each activity is related to how peace and violence or war impact a child's daily life directly. Television, toys, play activities, and personal heroes all play an intimate role in children's lives. An awareness of the peacefulness or violence inherent in each of these is an important step as a young peacemaker puts his or her "own house in order."

Television has long been criticized for its violence. Numerous studies have resulted in rather ambiguous findings, but the conclusion by most researchers is that TV violence has the most impact on children who come from violent homes or environments, or on children whose parents simply neglect to communicate any values. It has been concluded that responsible parents watch TV with their children, point out what is happening, help children label various behaviors, and state their values concerning those behaviors. The TV activity here attempts to help build these skills in children.

War toys and violent play have not been researched as much as TV, but it could be assumed that the effect would be similar to TV: children from violent homes or environments are likely to experience the most negative effects from such toys. Once again the activities help children to label the characteristics of toys and, assuming they are committed to becoming peacemakers, encourage them to make choices about toys they will keep and play in which they will participate.

Heroes are a big part of the lives of children. The worship of superheroes helps them build a feeling of control in a world in which they often have limited power. Children are encouraged here to consider definitions of heroism. It is hoped that they will realize that heroism is not restricted to Masters of the Universe, Superman, and Wonder Woman. Perhaps they will learn that such characters are not really so heroic at all. They are encouraged to begin learning about and identifying with peace heroes, so it is important that the stories and instruction here be made as concrete, realistic, and relevant as possible.

Objectives

For Young Children:
- To correctly label some acts of physical violence and some acts of support on TV.
- To state why some programs are not helpful for people to watch.
- To identify some war toys and war play.
- To list several exciting themes for play that are not violent.
- To recognize the names of four or five "peace heroes."

For Early Elementary Children:
- To correctly label most acts of physical violence, some psychological violence, and most support on TV.
- To rate a TV program's desirability for a peacemaker.
- To correctly label war toys and war play, and to identify when neutral toys are being used for war play.
- To build at least one dramatic play environment not involving war.
- To briefly describe four or five "peace heroes."

For Later Elementary Children:
- To analyze a TV program in terms of physical and psychological violence and acts of support.
- To register their opinions about programming with the programmers.
- To dispose of war toys.
- To identify nonviolent play activities which can fairly directly substitute for war play.
- To build a repertoire of nonviolent dramatic play ideas and environments.
- To state some details about the lives of four or five "peace heroes."

For All Children:
- To become critical TV and toy consumers.
- To experience the fun and excitement of nonviolent play.
- To begin to build a peace vocabulary including major historical figures.

TV Survey

You Will Need:

           • paper   • crayons, markers, or pencil   • a TV

What To Do:

1. Think about how you have seen people hurt each other on TV. It can be physical, something that hurts another person's body, like hitting or shooting. It also can be emotional, things that people say or do that hurt another person's feelings or how they feel about themselves.

2. Now think about how you have seen people help or support each other on TV. Support can be giving people something they need, telling them something helpful, caring about them, or helping them find someone else who can be helpful.

3. Get a piece of paper ready to be a checklist. Draw two lines from the top to the bottom to make three parts of your paper. At the top of one part write Physical Hurts, the next part should be called Emotional Hurts, and the third part should be called Support. Or draw pictures to remind you what each part means.

4. Pick a TV show to watch. It could be a cartoon, a movie, or a "sitcom." Just make sure it is a show you are allowed to watch. Watch the show for 15 minutes or a half hour. Make a check mark every time you see an act of support or violence.

5. Try this for different shows on different stations. You may want to ask your parents or teacher to do this also and compare your lists. Or work together with a friend or grown-up.

Let's Talk About It:

Talk about what you saw. How did it make you feel? Did the show make the violence seem okay or did it show people being sad about it? Did it show more violence or support? How is watching violence on TV different from what it would be like for real?

Other Things To Do:

Watch commercials and see what kinds of violence and support they show. Look at commercials for the army and other parts of the armed services. What do they show? Do they show any violence?

O Write letters to your TV stations to tell them what you think about certain TV shows and violence on their station. Ask your friends and family to write letters with you.

Try to go one day or one week without watching any TV. Think of other fun things to do. Be sure to spend some time as a family. Does TV keep families apart or bring them together?

War Toy Free Zone

You Will Need:

- paper
- crayons or markers
- a trash container

What To Do:

1. Look at the toys you like to play with and think about what you like about them.

2. Decide if you want to make your house or school or church a "War Toy Free Zone" by getting rid of toys that are only for playing war or fighting.

3. You may want to make rules that say you may not use other toys for playing war.

4. Make a sign for your "War Toy Free Zone" with a picture or words and post it on the door.

Let's Talk About It:

Do you have any toys which are good only for playing war? Which toys can be used both for playing war and in other ways?

What's fun about playing war? What's not fun about playing war? Why?

What makes some toys better than others? Do you ever get toys that fall apart right away? Are there some toys that are hard to play with without having problems or getting into fights? Why? What do you think "junk toys" could be?

Other Things To Do:

O Visit toy stores in your town and make a list of all the war toys sold there. Talk or write a letter to the store manager about how you feel about their choice of toys to sell.

O Make a list of good toys for kids. Include lots of different kinds of toys. Think of things that are safe, fun, can be played with in lots of different ways, can be played with by lots of kids or only a few, and are not for playing war. Include things for playing inside and out, for building, for doing art projects, games, toys for pretending, dolls and stuffed animals, and so on. Share your list with others.

O Start a "War Toy Free Zone" campaign in your community. Your friends can join you by getting rid of their violent toys, too. Share your good toys ideas with your friends when they make out Christmas lists and wish lists for parents and grandparents.

I Ain't Gonna Play at War No More

You Will Need:
- dress-up clothes
- "stuff"
- your imagination

What To Do:

1. Make a list of lots of interesting and exciting things you can play that are not playing war. You might include things like:

firefighters	pioneers	sports players	hospital
space explorers	racers	rescue workers	forest rangers

2. Choose what you would like to play and collect the things you will need, like hoses, boxes, "moon" rocks, sticks, animals, dress-up clothes, and other things. Put them together in a box.

3. Get together with your friends and play with your new "prop box."

Let's Talk About It:

Think of ways some children might think war play can be fun. Are the other games you thought of fun in some of the same ways?

What if a friend suggests you play war together? What could you say or do?

How do "props" help you play?

Other Things To Do:

A Go to the library to get more ideas for exciting things to play. Read books from the library about people's lives you are interested in.

Peace Heroes Book

Ghandi

You Will Need:
- paper
- crayons or markers

What To Do:
1. Think about what the word "peace" means. Make a list of people you know or have heard of that work for peace.

2. Draw pictures or cut out pictures of peace heroes working for peace. Show how they "saved the day" using peace. Write or have someone write your thoughts or a story at the bottom of your pictures.

3. Make a cover and collect your pages into a book of peace heroes.

Jane Addams

Let's Talk About It:
What is a hero? Do heroes need to hurt each other or have power over others?
What can people do to work for peace?
Who is your favorite peace hero? Why? What can you do to be more like that person?

Pete Seeger

Other Things To Do:
Learn about people throughout history that have worked for peace. You might want to learn about Ghandhi, Jane Addams, Martin Luther King, Jr., Mother Teresa, Harriet Tubman, Pete Seeger and others. Go to the library or ask someone to tell you more about them.
Invite someone in your town who works for peace to talk with your class or your family about his or her work for peace.
Make posters of your favorite peace heroes.

11
Peace Heroes to the Rescue

Background information:

While the previous chapter focused on personal peace activism, this chapter moves toward more public activism. Children will have the opportunity to explore how working with others to create murals and posters, to express their opinions on public issues, and to organize marches can magnify an individual's efforts.

Middle childhood has been called the "gang age." Joining clubs and getting involved in rituals and traditions are favorite activities for these children. Connecting this natural tendency toward groups and enthusiasm with peace work to create peace projects can plant and nurture seeds of personal commitment that could flourish for a lifetime.

The peace march has been an important tool for peacemakers for many years. This activity in this chapter provides an opportunity for children to explore the meanings and experiences of peace marches.

The peace mural builds on many of the activities in previous chapters, but adds a broadly cooperative effort and an activism focus. The same is true of the daydreaming activity.

Objectives

For Young Children:
- To learn some simple methods for expressing peace values.
- To recognize the term "peace march."
- To use their imaginations to think about peace.

For Early Elementary Children:
- To use art and other simple symbolic activities to express ideas about peace.
- To describe some motivations and experiences of peace marchers.
- To express some of their personal dreams for a peaceful world.

For Later Elementary Children:

- To organize friends to carry out peace activities.
- To use art and other symbolic expressions of ideas to communicate with a larger group.
- To describe some details about historic peace marches and marchers.
- To explain the relationship between dreaming and activism for improving the world.

For All Children:

- To work cooperatively with others in peace activities.
- To begin to learn that they are not alone in wanting peace.
- To build on the awareness and concern created by activities in previous chapters by telling others how they feel about peace.

Those Feet Were Made for Walkin'

You Will Need:
- a very long piece of paper
- paint in pie pans
- newspapers
- dishpans of soapy and plain water
- towels
- two chairs

What To Do:

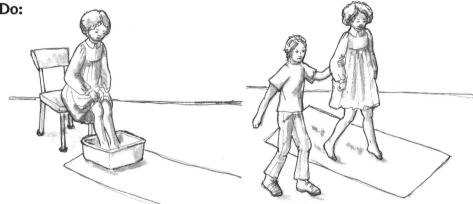

1. Put the pans with paint and one chair at one end of the long paper. Put the dish pans and another chair at the other end. (If you are indoors, put plenty of newspapers under the long paper.)

2. Sit on the first chair and put both feet in the paint. Then walk from one end of the paper to the other. Have someone hold your hand. Painted feet can be slippery!

3. Sit on the chair at the other end and step in the pan of soapy water. Swish them around to wash your feet. Step in the plain water to rinse them. Dry them with the towels. Have everyone else take a turn.

4. Let your picture dry. Hang it on a wall to remind you to keep walkin' the road for peace!

Let's Talk About It:

Why do people walk or march for peace? When do they do it?

Have you had any experiences like that to share?

Other Things To Do:

Have each person make an individual set of footprints.

Make a name for your poster. Take your "walkin' poster" and/or other posters on a peace walk or march.

Learn about some of the Great Peace Marches in history.

A Get books from the library about people who have spent many hours and years of their lives walking for peace, like Gandhi, Martin Luther King, Jr., Peace Pilgrim, the great Peace Marchers, Mother Teresa, and many others. Talk with people in a peace group in your town about their walks for peace.

A Plan a peace walk for your family, class, or friends. Plan where you will walk. Make signs or carry your "walkin' poster" on your walk. Be careful of traffic and other people.

Peace Mural

You Will Need:

- an old sheet (solid color)   • water color markers

What To Do:

1. Bring together a few or a lot of friends and family members. Have people draw pictures of peace and beauty on the sheet. Use many colors. Fill the whole sheet.

2. Hang your mural someplace that it can be shared with others.

Let's Talk About It:

What things are important to you that you would like to see on the peace mural?
How could you show those things? What pictures or symbols could you use?
Where could the mural be hung? Why would that be a good place?

Other Things To Do:

Set up tables with a sheet and markers at any kind of gathering of people. It could be a
    school or church meeting, a retreat, a family reunion, or whatever. Invite grown-ups
    and children to draw their ideas of peace on the sheet.
Learn the word "peace" in many different languages. Include these words on your
    mural.
A Make a quilt out of squares that individuals or families have made. The pictures on
    the squares can be made out of fabric crayons, embroidery, or acrylic paint. Each
    square could show something about peace. A grown-up can sew the squares
    together.

Pictures That Talk

You Will Need:
- drawing paper
- crayons, markers, or paint
- envelopes and stamps

What To Do:
1. Talk about some things you think are important. Some things to think and talk about are nature, friendship, families or children, conflict and war, or peace.

2. Make pictures that show what you think.

3. You might want to show your picture somewhere. Or you could send it to someone—a child nearby or far away, someone in the hospital or nursing home, the Mayor, the President. Think of someone you would like to tell what you think and send them a picture.

Let's Talk About It:
Why is it important for people to tell others what they think and how they feel? How can pictures show other people what you think?

If you decide to send your pictures to someone, why do you want that person to know what you think? What do you think he or she will do when the picture arrives?

What are other ways to show or tell people what you think?

Other Things To Do:
Tape record your ideas. Send the tape to someone or keep it for listening later.

Write a letter to someone about your ideas. If you cannot write by yourself, an adult can write the words for you. Some children may want to write to the leaders of the United States or the U.S.S.R. Their addresses are:

The President of the U.S.	The Premier of the U.S.S.R.
The White House	The Kremlin
Washington, D.C.	Moscow, U.S.S.R.

A Get the name of a child from another country you could write to as a pen pal. Ask your librarian, teacher, pastor, or someone from another country for a name or join a "twinning" project like Project MADRE, 853 Broadway, Room 301, New York, NY 10003, a project which pairs young children in the U.S. with children in Nicaragua.

Peacemakers are Dreamers, Too

You Will Need:

- markers or crayons   • paper   • brain power

What To Do:

1. Be very still. Take long, slow, deep breaths. Try not to think about the things around you.

2. Close your eyes and daydream about peace. Think about peace inside yourself, when you feel good inside. Think about peace between people, when people love and help each other. Think about peace between countries, when countries do not have to have guns and bombs and can be helpful instead. Try to imagine what it would be like to live in a family, school, neighborhood, or world that is peaceful. All problems are handled in a kind way. All people have the things they need.

3. Tell others what you think that kind of world would be like.

4. Draw a picture of the peaceful world you see.

Let's Talk About It:

What is peace like? What things would be different in a peaceful world?
Why is it important for peacemakers to use their imaginations?

Other Things To Do:

Using your ideas about a peaceful world, make up a play to share with others. Decide how many people you will need and who they should pretend to be. What things or props will you need and what scenery?

12

Holidays, Giving Days

Background information:

Holidays are special times for children and families. Unfortunately, the celebration of most holidays has become dominated with the advertising and sale of gifts and prepackaged foods, costumes, and decorations. The focus on purchasing the latest gadget or fashion overshadows the traditions and meanings of the holidays.

Another concern about holidays is related to their being a special time for families. Those without families or far away from other family members often feel very alone and empty at those times. What a wonderful opportunity for young peacemakers to have an impact!

This chapter is written in a slightly different format. Rather than describing a specific activity, it lists numerous ideas which can be adopted as desired. Hopefully the ideas will serve as inspiration for even further creativity.

Happy Holidays!

Objectives

For Young Children:
- To understand the meaning of some major holidays.
- To realize that holiday celebrations do not require purchased items.
- To identify family traditions related to holidays.

For Early Elementary Children:
- To state the important values celebrated by several major holidays.
- To learn that holiday celebrations vary in different countries and subcultures.
- To personally create a portion of a holiday celebration.

For Later Elementary Children:

- To plan and carry out several activities appropriate to a holiday and its values.
- To describe some holiday traditions in some other cultures.
- To design ways to include others in holiday celebrations.

For All Children:

- To think about people who are lonely and in need at holiday times.
- To use their creativity to create a holiday celebration.

Halloween

What To Do:

I. Costumes:
Make your own costumes using dress-ups, paper bags, boxes, fabric scraps, or whatever. Easy makeup:

1. Blend 2 tsp. shortening, 5 tsp. cornstarch, and 1 tsp. flour.

2. Add glycerin until creamy.

3. Add food coloring if colored makeup is desired.

4. Peanut butter or shredded coconut may be used for facial texture.

5. Brown clown makeup can be made by mixing 1 tsp. white shortening with 2½ tsp. cocoa.

(Do not leave it on very long. Some children may be allergic.)

II. Parades:
Have a Halloween parade for a group of people who may be lonely, like senior citizens, people in a nursing home, or people in a hospital.

III. Parties:
Join with another class, family, or group for a cooperative parade or party. Have an "everyone wins" costume contest.

IV. Trick-or-treating:
Trick-or-treat for UNICEF. Or trick-or-treat in a hospital or nursing home where you give treats away instead of getting them.

V. Pumpkins:
Have a jack-o-lantern decorating party. Scoop out the seeds, wash and dry them, and put them on an oiled cookie sheet. Bake the seeds with some salt at 375° for 30 minutes or until golden brown. They make a tasty snack! Cook the parts of the pumpkin that you cut out. Or just decorate the outside so that you can cook the whole pumpkin after Halloween. Give away pumpkins to friends or neighbors who do not have them.

Let's Talk About It:
What makes Halloween fun for you? How can you share the fun with others?

What is an "everyone wins" contest? How can you organize one? Why is it important for everyone to win?

Thanksgiving

What To Do:

I. Thankfulness:

1. Think about those things that are important to you and the things you wish for every person on the earth.

2. Make a picture or poster of things for which you are thankful. You can do this as a cooperative project, also.

II. Food:

1. Learn about good nutrition, which foods our bodies need and which foods are better to avoid.

2. Participate in a world hunger project.

3. As a family or other group, avoid junk food for one month. Save the money you would have spent on junk food and send it to a group working to stop hunger. Take up a food collection for your local "food bank" or soup kitchen.

III. Families:

1. Learn about your family's traditions at Thanksgiving time. What did your parents or grandparents do at Thanksgiving when they were young? Why does your family do what it does?

2. Talk about what you enjoy about your family.

3. Make your family tree. Who is in your family? Why are they important? You may want to learn more about your extended family also.

IV. Native Americans:

1. Learn about Native American Indians. Go to the library and study one or more tribes. Talk with Native American friends in your community. Ask about the traditions, religion, stories, song and dances, food, transportation, and other special things.

2. Plan some activities that you learned about and that interest you.

3. Learn about the problems facing Native Americans today.

Let's Talk About It:

Why do people think about world hunger at Thanksgiving time? Why do people think of Thanksgiving as a special family time?

Talk about the story of the pilgrims and Indians. Why do some people think it is an unfair story?

Christmas

What To Do:

I. Sharing money and things:
Give money or new or used items to your local Christmas bureau, Salvation Army, Toys for Tots program, Adopt-a-Family, or other group. They may collect toys, clothing, blankets, food, and other items for people in need.

II. Sharing happiness:
Plan or join in a caroling party, sharing your singing with neighbors or people in a nursing home or hospital. Think of other ways to give happiness. Some people are especially lonely at this time of year.

III. Sharing friendship:
Think about neighbors, friends, or people in your church or school who appreciate your friendship. Send cards, visit, or share Christmas treats. You may want to bake plates of cookies to take to your senior neighbors.

IV. Gifts:
Make your own simple gifts instead of spending lots of money. You could make:
1. placemats: drawings covered with clear contact paper;

2. T-shirts: use fabric crayons, permanent markers, or tie-dye;

3. bookmarks or cards: with your own drawings or paintings;

4. wall hangings: burlap and collage materials sewn with yarn;

5. puppets;

6. pictures, paintings, or drawings;

7. a coupon book: for hugs, backrubs, washing dishes, or helping in other ways; or

8. photos of yourself (especially for parents, grandparents, or teachers).

V. Wrapping paper:
Make your own wrapping paper. Use art work you have done, like pictures or drawings. Or recycle paper bags by drawing pictures or designs on them or making sponge paint prints. For small packages paper towels or napkins can be folded up and the ends dipped in food colors. Unfold and let dry.

VI. Religious celebrations:
Learn about the first Christmas. Why is it important to your family or church? Join in observing religious traditions. Ask questions about them.

Let's Talk About It:

Talk about lots of ways you can give happiness to others at Christmastime.

Why is it important to think of Christmas as a time of giving instead of just getting? How can you remind yourself and others about giving? What family traditions could you start to show how important giving is?

Do stores and TV commercials make you think about giving or getting? Why? What do your friends think about it?

Martin Luther King

I Have A DREAM

Martin Luther King Jr.'s Birthday

What To Do:

1. Learn about King:
Read about Martin Luther King, Jr.'s life. Find out and talk about things like the marches, sit-ins, jail, non-violence, discrimination, and other important parts of his life. *O* Listen to one of his speeches.

2. Birthday celebration:
Plan a birthday celebration to remember Martin Luther King, Jr. Make a birthday cake. Decorate it to show some of the important things to remember on this day.

3. Party activities:
Plan activities for your party and for the whole month of January. Some ideas are:
— singing songs of peace and justice;
— having each person share his or her dream of peace and justice; or
— writing letters telling what you like about Martin Luther King, Jr.'s ideas and actions and how things have changed because of his life and work.

4. Community events:
Attend a local community event celebrating the life of Martin Luther King, Jr. Write to the Martin Luther King, Jr. Center for Nonviolent Social Action, 449 Auburn Avenue, N.E., Atlanta, Georgia 30312, for more ideas.

5. Learn about other outstanding black women and men:
Read and learn about other black people that have made great contributions to our world.

6. Talk with other people:
Talk with friends or other people in your area: black, white, young, and old. Ask what King's birthday means to them.

Let's Talk About It:
How has Martin Luther King, Jr.'s life changed the world?
What was his dream? What dreams and wishes do you have for the world?
How can you help to make his dream and yours come true?

Valentine's Day

What To Do:

1. Cards
Make your own valentine cards. They can be simple with colored paper or drawings or they can be fancy with other collage materials like tissue paper, tiny beads or glitter, fabric scraps, doilies, or other materials.

2. "Adopted" grandparents:
Send valentines to your adopted grandparent or a group of senior citizen friends. Do not forget the visits, hugs, and smiles, too!

3. Lonely people:
Send valentines to other people who are lonely and need some caring, like people who are sick, shut-in, or in prison.

4. Party or card exchange:
Plan a valentine card exchange or party with another group of children, perhaps a school for children with special needs or with a church or school with children of a different cultural or racial background. Keep in touch with each other and get together again!

Let's Talk About It:
What is love? What are some ways to show love? Why is it important to show love to others? Do you know of people who feel left out? How can you help to include them?

What are some ways you show love every day of the year?

Easter

What To Do:

1. Celebrate life:
Celebrate Easter as a new beginning, a time of spring and new life. Plant a garden, flowers, or bulbs. Learn about and watch for animal babies and birds returning from the south. Share flowers or plants with others.

2. Religious celebration:
Learn about your family or church's religious traditions at this time of year. Ask questions and talk about what is meaningful to you.

Go to a sunrise service at church. Or have your own service with your family. Include music and Easter stories. End with a special breakfast together.

3. Easter egg hunt:
Plan a cooperative Easter Egg Hunt. Maybe everybody could search and help younger children search. Then everyone would share the eggs equally. Or maybe all the people could have their own notes to follow or eggs with their names on them.

4. Easter baskets:
Make a basket of colored eggs or other goodies to share with a friend, young or old. Think about healthy goodies to include. Weave your own basket with colored paper, or recycle a fruit box.

Let's Talk About It:
What do you like about springtime?
How can celebrating Easter be joyful and meaningful without buying lots of things you see in stores?
Why do people go to church on Easter?

Chinese
New Year

Saint Lucia's Day
Sweden

Hanukkah

Traditional
Celebrations

Other Celebration Traditions

You Will Need:
- a library
- friends from other cultures or with other religious traditions

What To Do:
1. Ask your friends to share with you what holidays they celebrate and how they celebrate them. What do they do? What things do they use? What food do they eat? What music do they sing or listen to? Perhaps they will show you some of their celebration symbols or share a game or recipe with you.

2. *A* Look up books in the library about those holidays and others. How are some holidays you observe celebrated differently in other countries?

3. Ask your family about some holidays they or their parents or grandparents celebrated. Ask how they celebrated holidays differently.

4. Plan some activities that you can do to enjoy and appreciate other holiday celebrations.

Let's Talk About It:
How are the same holidays celebrated differently in different countries? What traditions, decorations, or songs are similar?
What holidays are celebrated in other countries, but not here?
What do you like best about the different celebrations?
What would you like to try?

Resource List

Making Peace

Books:

Abrams and Schmidt. *Peace is in Our Hands.* Jane Addams Peace Association, 1213 Race Street, Philadelphia, PA 19107. A resource unit for teachers of kindergarten and grades 1 to 6, 1974.

Adcock and Segal. *Play Together, Grow Together: A Cooperative Curriculum for Teachers of Young Children.* White Plains, NY: Mailman Family Press. 1983.

Alternatives. *Alternative Celebrations Catalogue.* Alternatives, P.O. Box 429, Ellenwood, GA 30049.

Australian Journal of Early Childhood: Peace Education Issue (December 1985). Australian Early Childhood Association, P.O. Box 105, Watson, A.C.T. 2602, Australia.

Carlsson-Paige, Nancy. *Helping Young Children Understand Peace, War, and the Nuclear Threat.* Washington, DC: National Association for the Education of Young Children, 1985.

Carlsson-Paige, Nancy, and Diane Levin. *The War Play Dilemma: Balancing Needs and Values in the Early Childhood Classroom.* Teachers College Press, 1987.

Cherry, Clare. *Think of Something Quiet: A Guide for Achieving Serenity in Early Childhood Classrooms.* Belmont, CA: David S. Lake, 1981.

Cloud, Kate, and others. *Watermelons Not War! A Support Book for Parenting in the Nuclear Age.* Philadelphia: New Society Publishers, 1984.

Crary, Elizabeth. *Kids Can Cooperate: A Practical Guide to Teaching Problem Solving.* Order from: Parenting Press, Suite 400, 7750 31st Avenue NE, Seattle, WA 98115, 1985.

Ecumenical Task Force on Christian Education for World Peace. *Try This: Family Adventures Toward Shalom.* Nashville, TN: Discipleship Resources (P.O. Box 840, Nashville, TN 37202), 1979.

Farns, Christine King. *Martin Luther King, Jr.: His Life and Dream.* Lexington, Mass.: Ginn and Co., 1986. (Elementary curriculum guide.)

Greiner, Rosmarie. *Peace Education: A Bibliography Focusing on Young Children.* 126 Escalona Drive, Santa Cruz, CA 95060, 1984.

Haessly, Jacqueline. *Peacemaking: Family Activities for Justice and Peace.* New York: Paulist Press, 1980.

Judson, Stephanie, Ed. *A Manual on Nonviolence and Children.* New Society Publishers, 4722 Baltimore Ave., Philadelphia, PA 19143, 1984.

Kreidler, William J. *Creative Conflict Resolution: More Than 200 Activities for Keeping Peace in the Classroom K-6.* Glenview, IL: Scott Foresman, 1984.

McGinnis, Kathleen and James. *Parenting for Peace and Justice.* Maryknoll, NY: Orbis Books, 1981.

McGinnis, Kathleen and James. *Christian Parenting for Peace and Justice Program Guide.* Nashville, TN: Discipleship Resources, 1981.

Peachey, J. Lorne. *How To Teach Peace to Children.* Scottdale: Herald Press, 1981.

Prutzman, P., Burger, M. L., Bodenhamer, G., and Stern, L. *The Friendly Classroom for a Small Planet.* Wayne, NJ: Avery Publishing Group, 1987 (Interim Edition).

Children's Books:

Baker, Betty. *The Pig War* (An "I Can Read" History Book).

Burns, Marilyn. *I Am Not a Short Adult! Getting Good at Being a Kid.*

O Coerr, Eleanor. *Sadako and the Thousand Paper Cranes.*

DeKay, James T. *Meet Martin Luther King, Jr.* (early elementary and up)

Domanska, Janina. *The Turnip.*

Dr. Seuss. *The Butter Battle Book, Horton Hears a Who,* and *How the Grinch Stole Christmas!*

Giles, Lucille. *Color Me Brown.* Illustrations by Louis F. Holmes. Distributed by the Martin Luther King, Jr. Center, 449 Auburn Avenue, N.E., Atlanta, GA 30312.

Heyward, DuBose. *The Country Bunny and the Little Gold Shoes.*

Hirsh, Marilyn. *I Love Hanukkah.*

Hogan, Jan. *Gladdys Makes Peace.*

Leaf, Munro. *The Story of Ferdinand.*

Lehn, Cornelia. *Peace Be With You.* (Short stories of historical peace heroes.)

Lionni, Leo. *Frederick* and *Swimmy.*

Moore, Joy Hofacker. *Ted Studebaker: A Man Who Loved Peace.*

Oppenheim. *On the Other Side of the River.*

Silverstein, Shel. *The Giving Tree* and *The Missing Piece.*

Thompson, Marguerite. *Dr. Martin Luther King., Jr.: A Story for Children.* (preschool age)

O Wahl, Jan. *How the Children Stopped the Wars.*

Zim, Jacob (Ed). *My Shalom, My Peace: Paintings and Poems by Jewish and Arab Children.*

Organizations:

American Friends Service Committee
1501 Cherry Street
Philadelphia, PA 19102

Brethren House Ministries
6301 56th Avenue North
St. Petersburg, FL
    Order "Celebrate Advent: Activities
        for Children and Parents."

Children's Creative Response to Con-
    flict Program
Fellowship of Reconciliation
523 N. Broadway
Nyack, NY 10960

Church World Service, a Division of
    the National Council of Churches
Director of Education
P.O. Box 968
Elkhart, IN 46515

Concerned Educators Allied for a
    Safe Environment
c/o Peggy Schirmer
17 Gerry Street
Cambridge, MA 02138

Educators for Social Responsibility
23 Garden Street
Cambridge, MA 02138

Grace Contrino Abrams
Peace Education Foundation, Inc.
P.O. Box 191153
Miami Beach, FL 33119

MADRE
853 Broadway
Room 301
New York, NY 10003
    Support for the women and
        children of Nicaragua, Day
        Care Twinning Program.

Martin Luther King, Jr. Center for
    Nonviolent Social Change
449 Auburn Avenue, N.E.
Atlanta, GA 30312
    Guidelines for celebrating the
        King holiday, children's books.

Namchi United Enterprises
P.O. Box 33852
Station D
Vancouver, B.C.
Canada V6J4L6
    Order *We Can Do It! A Peace
        Book for Kids of All Ages.*

National Coalition on TV Violence
P.O. Box 2157
Champaign, IL 61820

Peace Museum
430 W. Erie St.
Chicago, IL 60610
    (traveling hands-on children's
        peace exhibit)

Parenting for Peace and Justice
    Network
Institute for Peace and Justice
4144 Lindell, #400
St. Louis, MO 63108

Stop War Toys Campaign
Box 1093
Norwich, CT 06360

APPENDIX
Suggested Scripture Verses

Section I: Caring for the Environment

Genesis 1—Creation

Leviticus 25: 23—The land belongs to the Lord. You are strangers and guests.

Deuteronomy 8: 7-10—The Lord is bringing you into a good land.

Psalm 23—The Lord is my shepherd.

Psalm 24: 1-2—The earth is the Lord's.

Matthew 6: 25-30—Lilies of the field.

Matthew 13: 1-9 or Mark 4: 1-9 or Luke 8: 4-8—Parable of the seed and the sower.

Matthew 13: 31-32 or Mark 4: 30-32—Mustard seed.

Romans 14: 20—Do not, for the sake of food, destroy the work of God.

Section II: Understanding People

Deuteronomy 15: 4—Let there be no poor among you.

Psalm 41: 1-3—Regard for the lowly and poor.

Matthew 5: 43-46—Loving enemies.

Mark 8: 1-9 or John 6: 5-13—Feeding the multitude.

Luke 3: 10-11—Sharing food and clothing.

Luke 10: 29-37—Good Samaritan.

Romans 12: 10-18—Make hospitality your special care; make friends with the poor.

Romans 14: 15—Do not let what you eat cause the ruin of another.

Galatians 3: 28—There are no distinctions. All are one in Christ.

Section III: Making Peace

Leviticus 19: 9–15—Treat your neighbor with justice and mercy.

Isaiah 2: 4—Turn swords into ploughshares.

Isaiah 11: 6—The wolf shall dwell with the lamb.

Matthew 5: 3–14—The Blessed.

Matthew 5: 38–42—Turning the other cheek, going the extra mile.

Matthew 5: 43–48 or Luke 6: 27–35—Love your enemies.

Matthew 19: 13–15 or Mark 10: 13–16 or Luke 18: 15–17—Jesus blesses little children.

Matthew 25: 34–40—Caring for the hungry, sick, and in prison.

Romans 14: 19—Let us then pursue what makes for peace and mutual upbuilding.

1 Corinthians 13: 1–7—Love chapter.

Hebrews 13: 1–3—Remember those in prison.

James 1: 22–27—Be doers, not only hearers of the word.

James 2: 15–17—We must practice what we believe and preach.

Also various scriptures appropriate to the holidays.

Notes

Notes